PICKLES
THE WORLD CUP DOG
AND OTHER UNUSUAL
FOOTBALL OBITUARIES

PICKLES
THE WORLD CUP DOG
AND OTHER UNUSUAL
FOOTBALL OBITUARIES

PETER SEDDON

First published 2007 by Aurum Press Limited
7 Greenland Street
London NW1 0ND
www.aurumpress.co.uk

A catalogue record for this book is available from the
British Library.

ISBN-10: 1 84513 284 X
ISBN-13: 978 1 84513 284 2

1 3 5 7 9 10 8 6 4 2
2007 2009 2011 2010 2008

Designed by Peter Ward
Typeset in Adobe Jensen by M Rules
Printed and bound in Great Britain by
MPG Books, Bodmin

INTRODUCTION

When the Scottish writer Sir Walter Scott opined in verse in 1815 that 'Life is itself but a game of football' he became the first in a long line of observers to forge a metaphorical link between 'the world's greatest game' and the roller-coaster ride that is the very stuff of mortal existence. A football match kicks off with only one outcome certain – that like life itself it will be brought to a close at the allotted time, a moment all too often thrust upon us prematurely, with scant regard for our sensibilities, and when the stark realisation that it is all 'too late' becomes a grim reality. The game's vocabulary certainly provides regular intimations of mortality. The seconds 'tick away' while time is 'wasted'; goals are scored 'in the dying moments' or 'right at the death'; a team has one fleeting chance to 'stay alive' in the cup; every man summons his 'final ounce of strength' for a 'last-gasp' effort as 'the final whistle beckons' – then in an instant it is 'all over' and the 'post-mortem' begins.

Death of the more permanent kind bears in football a great deal of poignancy. The inexorable move from footballer to 'former footballer' is no easy passage – almost an interim-death in itself – but when a once-vigorous athlete becomes an 'ex-footballer' in the most final sense it is something particularly tragic, for then the youthfulness and vitality still so clear in the mind's eye are consigned at a stroke to history. The shock discovery of the body of Alan Ball in April 2007 shortly before this manuscript was completed was just such a moment – the youngest and bounciest member of England's 1966 World Cup winning team was taken away in an instant while tending a bonfire in his garden.

Ball's is one of the 220 or so obituaries in this volume. It is included not so much for his greatness as a player, but because his demise was so completely unexpected and unconventional – indeed, as the book's title indicates: 'unusual'. For the opposite reason his pre-eminent England colleague Bobby Moore – who died of cancer after a long illness – is not featured here. In his stead are more unlikely characters from 1966: Lonnie Donegan, who immortalised mascot World Cup Willie in song; Willie's gloriously eccentric human counterpart Ken Baily; and this volume's eponymous canine hero, Pickles the Dog.

This is not then a selection concerned with the giants of the game *per se*, but rather with the men and women – and a handful of God's creatures – who occupy an unlikely place in its rich folklore: those whose lives have been touched by football in an unexpected way, or who have achieved something in the game considered out of the ordinary, incongruous, or even faintly ludicrous.

Some of them attained high office: you will encounter three kings, one queen, a British Prime Minister, a secretary of state for the Colonies, a deputy governor of the Bank of England, the founder of a London Polytechnic (who died in his bath), an Admiral of the Fleet, an Eton College headmaster, and the Indian-born vice-president of the Shropshire Chess Association, who perished after an attack of gout secure in the knowledge that he had scored the England team's first ever goal.

Here are to be found the inventors of goal nets, shin guards, the referee's whistle and Bovril, as well as the only Romany gypsy to play for England, the Portland cement manufacturer who was 'the fastest dribbler of the day' but declined to play for his country, a chief sanitary inspector for Shrewsbury, the Irish linen magnate who conceived the

idea of the penalty kick, and the Benedictine nun in whose fair hand the recorded history of football in the English language first began.

In their midst are one murder victim, a lone assassin, and enough suicide cases to form the nucleus of a highly talented squad. There are three Victoria Cross holders, a professional violinist, two men who died insane after both playing for Derby County, the first Iraqi attached to a League side, a famous Test cricketer who passed off his syphilis as a 'mosquito bite in the groin area', and the England captain who became a wealthy 'coke dealer'.

Some of the deceased went to their graves having achieved something unique: Arthur Pember was the only FA president to fully ascend Mont Blanc; the 'occasionally erratic' full-back Charles King is commemorated by a stuffed owl; John Auger Dixon was the only dressmaker of note to play for England; and the popular entertainer Rod Hull's fall from the roof of his bungalow during a televised Manchester United game proved fatal. His beloved 'Emu' survived him.

There are names here too which ring with greater clarity in more familiar fields: Edward Elgar, the fair-weather devotee of Wolverhampton Wanderers; his fellow composer Shostakovich, an impassioned collector of match statistics; novelist J.B. Priestley, 'a hard-tackling full-back in my youth'; the grocery baron Sir Thomas Lipton – of tea fame – who was a World Cup pioneer; and the Lord Protector of the Commonwealth Oliver Cromwell – 'a chief match-maker at football' – who allowed the game to hamper his university studies!

In such an eccentric collection one would expect to find goalkeepers. Those selected try hard not to disappoint. The founder of the Scouting movement Lord Baden-Powell was prone to 'dervish leaps, a blood-curdling war whoop, and an odd sort of native dance' when between the posts. The hapless Charlie Bunyan, after letting in 26 goals in a single game, offered the candid opinion that he had actually played 'rather well'. The Blackburn Rovers custodian Herby Arthur faced Burnley entirely alone. Chic Brodie – who the *Sun* called 'a walking mishap' – had his career ended by an over-the-top challenge from a pitch-invading dog. And the Crystal Palace keeper Billy Callender hanged himself at Selhurst Park, although not, as has been said, 'from his own crossbar'.

The philosopher Albert Camus was a goalkeeper, so too the Russian émigré novelist Vladimir Nabokov. Another celebrated author, Sir Arthur Conan Doyle, also guarded the citadel sporadically. His is one of a number of obituaries which either expand upon or re-address what has become accepted wisdom. For example, the habitual assertion that Doyle 'turned out several times for Portsmouth FC' is dubious on two counts. He actually played for the amateur side Portsmouth AFC – a forerunner of the current club – and in fact made almost 80 appearances. Indeed, as a leading light in the team later dubbed 'the original Pompey' he played a significant part in establishing the association game in the naval port. What a great pity he neglected to imbue Sherlock Holmes with a similar passion, for the urgent exclamation 'Come Watson, the game's afoot' might then have taken on an entirely different meaning.

Many of the obituaries are selected in light-hearted spirit, and are intended to be read as such. I make no serious claim that Jack the Ripper has a profound connection to football, but he earns his obituary all the same for a serendipitous linkage to the game which is curiously diverting. Included likewise are P.G. Wodehouse, Henry VIII, Rudyard Kipling, Jean-Paul Sartre, and the 'revered fell-walker'

Alfred Wainwright, all of whose football credentials have been kept under wraps for far too long.

When Aurum published *Peter the Lord's Cat* – the cricketing equivalent of this volume – its compiler Gideon Haigh selected his splendid entries direct from the long-standing obituaries section of *Wisden*. Because football has no comparable source I have penned the obituaries retrospectively and with the benefit of hindsight, so have been able to place lives and events in context. The £1,000 transfer fee for Alf Common may have been considered 'disgracefully immoral' in 1905, but the figure now raises an eyebrow for very different reasons. So too the negotiated playing terms of the England winger Bobby Evans, who in lieu of travelling expenses when starting out in the game meekly accepted an allowance of 'two turnips a week'.

Pickles the World Cup Dog is not intended to be a conventional history of football, but the incidental by-product of the collective entries approximates to a timeline of the game's development. Edward II gains a place for his ban in 1314 of the 'rampaging pursuit of large footballs' in the streets of London. Five centuries later came the educated ranks of ex-public schoolboys who sanitised the game. Numbered amongst them are men of standing in society who made their mark on the association game early in its recorded history, such as Cuthbert John Ottaway, the first captain of England, said by the press to have died as a result of 'a night's dancing', a 'scurrilous accusation' vehemently denied by his family. The Reverend Walter Gilliat marked his sole England appearance by notching up a sublime hat-trick. The Wanderers stalwart Charles Absolom, a Test cricketer, in retirement adopted the life of a Red Indian – he later went to sea and was crushed to death under a wayward consignment of sugar cane.

They were followed by staunch pioneers like Llewellyn Henry Gwynne, who pursued the leather with religious fervour and was the only bishop to bag a double brace on Christmas Eve, and the first superstar professional to make himself a household name before the nineteenth century was out: the England striker Steve Bloomer, once a member of Gwynne's church choir team. The game has advanced relentlessly ever since and will go on doing so despite its occasional troubles.

Above all, then, this is a book about the joy of football in its widest sense. In *Association Football and the Men Who Made It* (1906) the game was described as 'a pervasive virus from which no man is immune'. Little has changed a century later – except the epidemic is now global and not restricted by gender. I will give the final word to the novelist Arnold Bennett – when one of his characters innocently questions 'what football has got to do with being mayor', the answer is delivered with perky sagacity: 'Football has got to do with everything.'

ABSOLOM, CHARLES ALFRED, who died in Trinidad on July 30, 1889, aged 43, was an exemplar of the early breed of gentleman pioneer who took to both football and cricket with equal alacrity. He was born at Blackheath, Kent, on June 7, 1846. On April 2, 1864 – 'before a goodly array of spectators' – he played against No Names of Kilburn in the historic first game of the Wanderers FC, the itinerant club later to win the FA Cup on five occasions. *Bell's Life* described the outset: 'By a happy acquaintance with the chief points of the art of tossing, as exemplified through the medium of a shilling piece, the choice of goal was won by the rovers, who, unwillingly as they always are to turn their backs on friend or foe, selected the upper goal, with the wind and sun behind them.'

Absolom cut a striking figure in the orange, violet and black outfit first worn by the Wanderers. He cultivated a monumental beard at least the equal of that worn by cricket's W.G. Grace, his fearsome demeanour earning him whilst at Trinity College the sobriquet 'the Cambridge Navvy'. He was also a fine cricketer – in his one Test for England (1879) he achieved a half-century against Australia, and also played for Cambridge University and Kent (1866–79), earning the distinction in 1868 of becoming the first man in first-class cricket to be given out for obstructing the field.

Charlie Absolom cut short his sporting career to travel. He became a ship's purser and in later years spent time in North America with the Red Indians. Few football practitioners endured such a distressing death. Whilst loading cargo in Port of Spain he was buried under a wayward consignment of sugar cane, the best part of life being crushed from him. Regardless of the commodity – for some assert it was bananas – witnesses to the grave

misfortune attested that Absolom suffered the cruellest agony. He
died in hospital two days later.

ADAMS, JAMES, the Scottish international right-back – 'whose crisp
tackling won applause even in away games' – died aged 78, on April
24, 1943, in New Jersey, United States, where he had emigrated. In
three Scotland appearances (1889–93) he was always victorious,
enjoying with but little exertion an aggregate return of 19 goals to 2.

Born in Edinburgh in 1864, he won the Scottish Cup with
Hearts in 1891. After moving to Everton (1894 and 1895) he
returned to Hearts to end his career. Although one of their finest
backs it is ironic that in 1894–95 – the season in which Adams was
first absent from his customary station – Hearts won their first
Scottish League title while Everton could finish only runners-up in
England.

Prior to his English sojourn James Adams secured a lasting
place in football's timeline for an unsavoury incident which altered
the laws of the game. When he punched out an opponent's goal-
bound shot during an 1890–91 Cup tie, the resultant furore led to
the Scottish FA introducing penalty kicks. After several penalties
were erroneously awarded before the innovation became law, the
world's first conversion of a 'legal' penalty kick finally occurred
when Alex McColl scored for Renton in their 3–2 win at Leith
Athletic on August 22, 1891.

Adams's reaction to having spawned such a dramatic device
did not survive him, but that he should thereafter be responsible
for the first ever penalty conceded by Hearts may be considered
poetic justice. In retirement he became a qualified referee, and by
his death had long worked in America as a stonemason.

ADOLPH, PETER ARTHUR, born in Brighton in 1916, an only child,
died aged 78 in 1994. In August 1946 – while living with his
widowed mother in Langton Green, near Tunbridge Wells,

Kent – he applied for a patent on a table football game he had devised. When his intended name 'The Hobby' was vetoed by the Patent Office he instead used part of the Latin name for the hobby falcon – *Falco Subbuteo* – a mischievous nod to his passion for ornithology.

In 1968 the games company Waddington paid Adolph £232,000 for his globally successful 'Subbuteo' business. The proceeds permitted him to indulge his unlikely twin passions – his collection of rare birds' eggs, once described as 'the envy of the British Museum', and his array of American cars, which included a gold Pontiac Firebird and a Chevrolet convertible. Prior to making his fortune Adolph was employed in the accounts department of a processed meat company, and by the Pensions Office in London. He also sold birds' eggs by mail order.

As befits a lifelong supporter of Queen's Park Rangers, his funeral was adorned by a three-foot-high wreath in the shape of a Subbuteo figure in QPR kit. His life is celebrated in *Growing up with Subbuteo* (2006) by his son Mark. The game's trademark 'Flick to Kick' slogan remains an iconic catchphrase.

ALLISON, JOHN, the former director and chairman of Manchester City FC, died in Manchester on April 14, 1919, taking his place in the pantheon of football history for his pioneering methods in the treatment of injuries.

He was born in the village of Holloway, Derbyshire, in 1853. It was said that another local resident, Florence Nightingale, inspired him to pursue a career in health care. After studying massage in Sweden and Philadelphia, in the USA, he set up a small practice in Manchester before an ironic stroke of luck – a patient died and left him a large legacy – enabled his expansion. With the windfall he set up a hydropathic establishment 'for the treatment of muscular and limb injuries' at Hyde Road, Ardwick, close to the ground of newly formed Ardwick FC, the club destined to become Manchester City.

By the 1890s 'Allison's Football Hospital' had become the establishment of choice for the leading professional clubs. Hitherto a brisk rub with a coarse towel had been thought the most efficacious treatment for muscle injuries, but Allison's vigorous use of the Swedish vibrator, along with a range of water and heat treatments, and pulley-operated weight systems, revolutionised thinking. Such methods paved the way for the centre at Lilleshall, Shropshire, which would rehabilitate later generations of players.

John Allison had a strong interest in many sports and was president of the Salford Harriers Athletics Club. When football's 'Father of Fitness' died aged 66, many in the game noted his passing with more than a twinge of sadness.

ANDERSON, ALFRED, a World War One veteran born in Dundee on June 25, 1896, died 'Scotland's oldest man' at the Mundamalla Nursing Home, Newtyle, on November 21, 2005. At 109 years he was the last surviving veteran to have heard the guns of the Western Front fall silent during the celebrated Christmas Day truce of 1914. He could recount from personal experience (the last man living able to do so) how on that occasion British and German troops played impromptu football games in no-man's-land – although admitting in a droll interview when aged 108 that he did not take part as he was 'resting at the time'.

The truce has been termed 'a poignant interlude of civility during a time of unrelenting carnage' and Anderson gave tangible evidence of one of football's greatest folk tales, which has been both celebrated and fantastically embellished through song, story, film and dubious reminiscences. The 1990 song by The Farm – 'All Together Now' – was inspired by the truce and became an anthem for the English game.

Private Alf Anderson of the Fifth Battalion Black Watch was awarded the French Légion d'honneur in 1998 and his biography

A Life in Three Centuries was published in 2002. He was by profession a joiner and until six weeks before his death lived independently. A spokesman for the Royal British Legion said: 'He was our last surviving link with a time that shimmers on the edge of our folk memory.' A bronze bust of the veteran is in the Black Watch Museum in Perth.

ARLOTT, LESLIE THOMAS 'JOHN', OBE, died at his home on Alderney, the Channel Islands, on December 14, 1991, at the age of 77. Familiar to the public as John Arlott he was many things – poet, author, wine connoisseur and broadcaster – but was best known as 'The Voice of Cricket' for his lyrical commentaries on BBC radio (1946–80). He had a less-publicised long love affair with football, a passion he maintained from boyhood until the 1970s, when the 'modern game' jilted him, and he it.

Born in Basingstoke, Hampshire, on February 25, 1914, he became a boyhood supporter of Reading, cycling the 34-mile round journey to admire his heroes. He was soon performing lustily for his school – Queen Mary's in Basingstoke – first at full-back and later as a rampaging centre-forward, describing himself as 'strong but lumpen and very prone to clumsiness'. That proved his undoing – after clattering into a goalkeeper he was informed by his headmaster that he had 'disgraced the school's name' and would 'never be selected again'.

In the 1930s when serving in the Hampshire police force he began to follow Southampton and had risen to the rank of sergeant before discovering his true vocation in 1946. Of his many football commentaries for radio most are lost, but his trademark imagery survives in copious match reports – for the *Guardian*, *Observer*, *Evening News*, *The Times* and *News Chronicle* – many written under the *nom de plume* 'Silchester'. Eddie Baily of Spurs was described as 'neat as a trivet, busy as a one-man band, alert as a boarding-house cat, and as elusive as a dog in a fair' – and

Arsenal were caustically labelled 'something of a test case in rough play'.

But for a twist of fate he might have perished in the 1958 Munich air crash. Designated to fly with Manchester United to Belgrade he was replaced at the eleventh hour by the more senior reporter H.D. 'Donny' Davies, who lost his life. Arlott instead received a telephone call – while browsing in a London book-shop – instructing him to pen the obituaries of those who died. He completed the harrowing task with great compassion and a lasting tinge of guilt.

Manchester United were later implicated in his final split with the game – he had already wavered – for twice in his sixties he was attacked on trains by groups of their fans. In the worst incident he received a knuckleduster plum in the face, a blow he countered by smiting the youth over the head with a bottle of claret. Unnerved and disillusioned in equal part he declared his football reporter days at an end in 1973–74.

He retired to Alderney in 1980 – the island he called 'one of the most felicitous environments in the British realm' – and his grave there in St Ann's churchyard carries two lines of his own poetry: 'So clear you see those timeless things ... That, like a bird, the vision sings.'

ARTHUR, WILLIAM JOHN HERBERT, the goalkeeper known as 'Herby', was born in Blackburn on February 14, 1867, and died on November 27, 1930. In seven England games (1885–87) he let in four goals but was never on the losing side. With his sole first-class club Blackburn Rovers (1880–92) he completed a remarkable hat-trick of FA Cup wins (1884–86) and was said to be 'quite brilliant, cool in action and always clearing his lines with despatch'.

He is famous for the unique occasion he unwittingly became a 'one-man team'. In arctic conditions at Burnley in December 1891, Blackburn fell 3–0 in arrears by half-time. Following the break the Rovers' ranks resumed play with marked reluctance, and shortly after the restart all their outfield players departed the field complaining of the bitter cold. The abandoned goalkeeper was left to hold the fort single-handed.

The referee – the notorious FA official J.C. Clegg (Sheffield) – insisted the game should proceed. As the Burnley men bore down on Arthur's goal an injudicious pass presented the canny Blackburn keeper with an opportunity to scream 'Offside!' Referee Clegg rightly upheld the claim, but with not a soul to pass to from the resulting free kick the lonely Arthur dallied for such an eternity that the nettled arbiter had to abandon the game. Two days later, when Rovers played Sunderland, the doughty net-minder was given a benefit for his 'loyalty in extremis'. Herby Arthur became a commercial traveller and by the time of his death aged 63 had dined well on the tale for many years.

ASHTON, ACTING SQUADRON LEADER CLAUDE THESIGER, who was born in Calcutta, India, on February 19, 1901, was killed aged 41 in an air accident over Caernarfon, Wales, on October 31, 1942, whilst serving in the Royal Air Force. An amateur all-rounder of the old school, he captained Winchester College at football, cricket, rackets and fives, and at Cambridge University (1921–23) won blues in soccer, hockey and cricket. He appeared in most positions for the crack amateurs Corinthians, and remains the last footballer to captain England in his only full international appearance, against Northern Ireland in Belfast in October 1925. He was selected at centre-forward, despite it being said previously that 'his only real weakness is in headwork'. His best position was considered to be half-back.

The youngest of three sons of Hubert Shorrock Ashton – each of them county cricketers – Claude played 89 times for Essex (1921–38). This number would have been higher but for his professional commitments as a chartered accountant.

The tragedy which caused Ashton's death deprived the world of two sporting talents. The aircraft piloted by the former England football captain collided with one being flown by the Surrey cricketer Roger de Winton Kelsall Winlaw. Both men perished simultaneously. Claude Ashton is buried at Fryerning, Essex, in St Mary's Church. Squadron Leader Winlaw's batting average was 35.63.

BADEN-POWELL, LORD ROBERT STEPHENSON SMYTH, a Boer War hero, prolific writer, and founder in 1908 of the world Scouting movement, died at Nyeri, Kenya, on January 8, 1941, aged 83. He was born in Paddington, London, on February 22, 1857. At Charterhouse School (1870–76) – where he was First XI goal-keeper – his eccentricities attracted an expectant gathering behind his goal. An Old Carthusian recalled: 'He was cool under pressure, and handled well, but had his own peculiar ways. He bellowed a constant stream of rather bizarre encouragement to his fellow players, and when faced by an advancing forward would make dervish leaps and let out a blood-curdling war-whoop in an effort to put him off. During slack periods of play he was given to performing a primitive sort of dance between his posts. And he always changed his boots at half-time.'

In *Scouting for Boys* (1908) Baden-Powell wrote: 'Football is a grand game for developing a lad physically and morally, for he learns to play with good temper and unselfishness, to play in his place and "play the game", and these are the best of training for any game of life.'

But he added a withering caveat denigrating professionalism:

> It is a vicious game when it draws crowds of lads away from playing the game themselves to be merely onlookers at a few paid performers. Thousands of boys and young men, pale, with narrow chests, hunched-up, miserable specimens, smoking endless cigarettes, numbers of them betting, all of them learning to be hysterical, as they groan or cheer in panic unison with their neighbours.

At Charterhouse – where he adopted the sobriquet 'Lord Bathing Towel' – a teacher remembered his former charge as 'an admirable madman'. Nor was his football prowess quickly forgotten – on returning to his school after an epoch-making stand at the Siege of Mafeking a banner of welcome proclaimed 'Goal well kept, B-P'. His three children and his wife Olave – the World Chief Guide, 32 years his junior – survived him.

BAILY, KENNETH HENRY HIGHETT, a former civil servant, Tory councillor, and official mascot to the England football team, lost his brave battle against liver cancer on December 10, 1993, aged 82, at the Bramley House Nursing Home in Bournemouth.

Born in Burnham-on-Sea, Somerset, on August 8, 1911, he became a notable athlete. In 1939 he tried to avert the onset of war by 'running across the Atlantic' – a non-stop relay around the decks of a liner – to present a petition to the United States president Franklin D. Roosevelt. More than half a century later the *Guinness Book of Records* noted that he had run 190,805 miles by his eightieth birthday.

As a younger man he was adept at football, squash, golf and hockey, and when retired took a daily dip in the sea and spent four hours a week ice skating. In his spare moments he rode his bicycle around Bournemouth – often in the guise of Winston Churchill or Haile Selassie.

On becoming mascot of Bournemouth FC in the 1950s he adopted the costume which became his trademark – a Union Flag waistcoat, scarlet tails, white gloves and a pith helmet, later replaced by a black topper. Extending his allegiance to the England team in the 1960s he attended all their games for three decades. He also became a well-known presence at FA Cup Finals, the Olympic Games, Wimbledon and important rugby matches – indeed it was Ken's flag that covered up the ample assets of the streaker Erika Roe at Twickenham in 1982.

His news credits were wide and varied. When out jogging one night in a luminous suit in 1958 he was attacked by an angry owl. He wrote for the *Bournemouth Times* under the pen-name 'Genevieve'. He was the only man to become both a freeman of Bournemouth and a Subbuteo figure. And in a celebrated encounter with royalty he was asked by Prince Charles, 'Where did you escape from?'

A lifelong bachelor – living with his mother in the same flat in Bournemouth for 56 years – he neither smoked nor drank: 'The ladies are all very well, but I'm in love with the flag you see. My only vices are coffee cream chocolates and trifle.' Charges of an alleged indecent assault of two boys in 1985 were dismissed. In support of the England football team he visited 40 countries and travelled almost 200,000 miles. After his death he was described as 'the most famous man in Bournemouth' and 'a football icon the like of which we will never see again'.

BAIRSTOW, DAVID LESLIE, who played 17 games in the Bradford City forward line in 1971–72, was discovered dead in Marton-cum-Grafton, North Yorkshire, on January 5, 1998, aged 46. He had hanged himself from the staircase at his home – severe financial troubles, an impending drink-driving charge, and concern for his wife Janet who was suffering from cancer were all blamed.

Born in Bradford on September 1, 1951, 'Bluey' was a better cricketer than footballer, enjoying four Tests for England and a long career with Yorkshire (1970–90). Along with Tommy Cook (q.v.) and Stuart Leary (q.v.) he therefore forms a triumvirate of the 'double breed' – first-class cricketers who were also professional footballers – to have died by their own hands.

Bairstow's obituary in *Wisden* recorded: 'He was loud, combative, and combustible, but the manner of his death stunned the game, for he had always seemed the most indomitable and least introspective of men.' His one goal for Bradford was unremarkable, but when keeping wicket for Yorkshire he once took a record 11 catches in a single match.

BALDERSTONE, JOHN CHRISTOPHER, one of the last men to play cricket and football at the highest level, died at his home in Carlisle on March 6, 2000, aged 59. He had been suffering from cancer. 'Baldy' was an inside-forward for Carlisle United – producing 78 goals in 429 games (1965–74) – and also served Huddersfield Town, Doncaster Rovers and Queen of the South. In his first-class cricket career (1961–86) with Leicestershire and Yorkshire he scored 19,034 runs, took 310 wickets, and played two Tests for England (1976). He later stood as a first-class umpire, enjoying the minor distinction of being the first third umpire used in the game.

In September 1975 he accomplished a unique dual appearance in a single remarkable day. He spent the early part in the field for Leicestershire against Derbyshire at Chesterfield, helping his team gain the required number of bowling points to secure the County Championship. In the afternoon he batted to 51 not out at the close of play. And later that evening he played for Doncaster Rovers in their home 1–1 draw against Brentford in the Football League. For good measure he returned to the cricket field the following day to complete a century and take three wickets.

At Carlisle United in 1974–75 he scored a penalty which took the team briefly to the top of the First Division before a drastic loss of form saw them relegated. Although born in Huddersfield – on November 16, 1940 – Chris Balderstone chose to retire to Cumbria less than a year before his end. An admirer said: 'He was a fine and positive player at our two great sports, and a gentleman in everything he did, both on and off the field. His death came as a great shock to his many friends.'

BALL, ALAN JAMES, MBE, the youngest member of England's 1966 World Cup-winning side, and the second of that team after the captain Bobby Moore in 1993 to die, was pronounced dead at his home in Warsash, Hampshire, in the early hours of April 25, 2007. The 61-year-old former Everton and Arsenal star had suffered a heart attack while attempting to quench a garden bonfire which had got out of hand.

Born in Farnworth, near Bolton, on May 12, 1945, he joined Everton from Blackpool in 1966 for a British record transfer fee of £110,000. After 208 League games and 66 goals he moved to Arsenal and then Southampton, before closing his career with shorter returns to Blackpool and Southampton, and finally a 17-game spell with Bristol Rovers in 1983.

In a ten-year England career (1965–75) the 'perpetual motion' midfielder won 72 caps for his country and scored eight goals. Red-haired and combative, he was blessed with both skill and vision, but at only 5ft 6in relied heavily on energy and tenacity, and was likened in one description to a Spitfire aeroplane, of which it was once written: 'There is something irresistibly endearing about a very small thing which fights like hell for its country.'

He became a manager, but at a string of clubs failed to emulate his success as a player, and retired from the game completely in 1999. In 2004 the loss of his wife Lesley to cancer badly affected him, but he had been planning new business ventures when his unexpected death occurred. His approach to both football and life was signified by his distinctive trademark autograph: 'Alan J. Ball – WIN.'

BALL, THOMAS EDGAR, the Aston Villa defender, was shockingly killed in the late evening of Sunday, November 11, 1923, aged 23, the day after making an outstanding contribution to his team's 1–0 away win at Notts County. Born in the small mining village of Usworth, County Durham, on February 11, 1900, he was briefly affiliated to Newcastle United before transferring to Villa in January 1920. He had played 74 League games when he was shot dead at his home in Brick Kiln Lane, Perry Barr, by his neighbour and landlord, the former policeman George Stagg. The confrontation had followed an argument about Ball's dog and chickens straying onto Stagg's land. At Stafford Assizes in February 1924 the 45-year-old Stagg was found guilty of 'wilful murder' and sentenced to hang. This was later commuted to penal servitude for life, and Stagg died in Highcroft Mental Hospital, Birmingham, on February 1, 1966, at the age of 87.

Tommy Ball is the only British professional footballer proven to have been murdered. He was survived by his wife Beatrice May, with whom he had shared a drink at the Church Tavern on the eve of the tragedy. He was buried in St John's Church Yard, Perry Barr, each corner of his grave being adorned by a stone football.

BARTHOLOMEW, JOHN ERIC, MBE, known by his stage name Eric Morecambe, was born on May 14, 1926, and died aged 58, on May 28, 1984, after suffering a heart attack following a theatre appearance in Tewkesbury.

A football enthusiast dubbed 'Mr Luton Town', he was first a director (1970–77) and then vice-president of the club. Via a series of contrivances he placed it on the map, famously persuading the serious actress Glenda Jackson to wield a Luton Town banner on the *Morecambe and Wise Show*, thus publicising the club to 20 million television viewers. When Luton won promotion to the First Division in 1974 Morecambe was photographed sharing a celebratory bath with the players while still wearing his suit.

With his comedy partner Ernie Wise he was the first to insert regular football gags into a television show. His involuntary shout of 'Arsenal' upon hearing a cough – ritually followed by 'Who said that?' – remains an enduring catchphrase. Occasional forays into 'serious' football broadcasting proved legendary, not least an appearance on *World of Sport* on Christmas Eve 1977 when regular presenter Dickie Davies was thoroughly upstaged.

On another occasion he delivered live commentary for BBC Radio 2: '0–0 at the moment, for Luton, and Luton have a free kick coming up now, which Bobby Thomson's going to take. Yes, Anderson, it's there, wa-hey, how about that . . . knockout – that's fabulous that!'

In *Over the Moon . . . Sick as a Parrot* – Morecambe's sartorial guide for England fans travelling to the 1982 World Cup in Spain – he appeared with an outsize pair of maracas complemented by long white shorts, string vest, garters, a knotted handkerchief, and a Bulldog Bobby rosette. His *Eric Morecambe on Fishing* – completed shortly before his death – reflected a further sporting passion.

A suite at Kenilworth Road – Luton's home ground – is named after him, and at his birthplace Morecambe, in Lancashire, a bronze statue commands the seafront. In 1999 a British internet poll voted Morecambe 'the funniest person of the 20th century'.

BASTARD, SEGAR RICHARD, the former association football referee, born at Bow, London, on January 25, 1854, died of a heart attack at Epsom station on March 20, 1921, aged 67. He first came to prominence as a 'knight of the whistle' at the 1878 Cup Final between Wanderers and Royal Engineers at the Kennington Oval, and at the same venue, on January 18, 1879, refereed the first ever England v. Wales international match.

Like many of his contemporaries he was both a player and an official at the same time, serving Corinthians as a guest and playing outside-right for the now defunct Upton Park. He was also a flank man for England against Scotland on March 13, 1880, when Scotland prevailed by five goals to four. Although said to have performed 'capitally' Bastard never played for England again.

He was a competent cricketer – assisting Essex before they became a first-class county (1881–85) – and a noted gambler, being a keen follower of the turf and one of the first footballers known to have owned a racehorse. By profession an attorney, he served on the FA Committee between 1877 and 1883. His father – also Segar Bastard – was a hop merchant.

BELL, 2ND LIEUT. DONALD SIMPSON, VC, a steady right full-back said to have 'played grandly' and 'covered well', was killed during the Battle of the Somme on July 10, 1916, close to Contalmaison, France, aged 25. The spot where he fell became known as 'Bell's Redoubt'. Five days earlier Bell – of the Ninth Battalion of the Yorkshire Regiment the 'Green Howards' – had shown conspicuous bravery at 'Horseshoe Trench' while attacking a German machine gun, for which action he was posthumously awarded the Victoria Cross.

Donald Bell was born in Harrogate, Yorkshire, on December 3, 1890. He attended Knaresborough Grammar School and in 1909 entered Westminster College, representing them at football, rugby, cricket, hockey and swimming.

While there he played football for Crystal Palace as an amateur. After taking a teaching post in Harrogate he joined the Football League club Bradford Park Avenue as a professional, playing five games in 1913–14.

When the outbreak of war in August 1914 curtailed his sporting ambitions, 'Donny' Bell speedily volunteered his services, earning the distinction of being the first professional footballer to enlist and the only English professional player awarded the Victoria Cross. Cricketing romantics suggest that Bell's bowling experience enabled him to throw grenades with unerring accuracy, but Bell adopted a stance more common to footballers – 'I just hit it' – for in his last letter to his mother, written shortly after his heroic strike, he said: 'I hit the gun first shot from about 20 yards. It was the biggest fluke alive. I did nothing. I only chucked one bomb, but it did the trick.' He signed off, 'I believe God is watching over me. It rests with him whether I pull through or not.'

On July 9, 2000, a memorial to Donald Simpson Bell was unveiled at 'Bell's Redoubt' and he is further honoured by a window in Westminster College's chapel. He was survived by his wife Rhoda Margaret, who he had married 36 days before his death.

BELL, HAROLD, an outstanding servant of his only club Tranmere Rovers, and who was born in Liverpool on November 22, 1924, died aged 69 in 1994. In a remarkable run of 401 consecutive League appearances from 1946 to 1955 the centre-half and captain established a Football League record which seems unassailable. Including cup ties he amassed a grand total of 459 successive appearances and by his retirement in 1959–60 had played 595 League games and scored 11 goals. His ashes were scattered on the Prenton Park pitch.

BENFIELD, SGT. THOMAS CHARLES, of the Leicestershire Regiment, last living in England at 31 Woodland Road, Leicester, died aged 29 in France on September 19, 1918, serving his country.

After entering the record books as a marksman he became the victim of one. On September 6, 1913 – playing for Leicester Fosse in a Division Two game against Arsenal at the London club's new stadium – he became the first man to score a goal at Highbury. The 'Gunners' rallied to emerge 2–1 victors.

On moving to Derby County the inside-forward's 15 goals helped them win the Second Division championship in 1914–15. Thereafter he was engaged in World War One, his life being ended by a German marksman's bullet. Curiously, his Derby County team-mate Lance Corporal George Brooks was killed in the same arena only 19 days later. Tommy Benfield scored 38 goals in 144 League games and was survived by his wife Elsie.

BENNETT, ENOCH ARNOLD, author, critic and journalist, died on March 27, 1931, aged 63. Born in Hanley, Stoke-on-Trent,

Staffordshire, on May 27, 1867, Arnold Bennett is among the few novelists whose incorporation of football into their works is not gratuitous. He expressed a genuine lifelong interest in sport and demonstrated a keen understanding of the importance of football in society.

Some of his earliest writings – under the byline 'Knotty Notes' – were his football articles in 1888 for the *Staffordshire Knot* newspaper. In *The Matador of the Five Towns* (1912) the title story features Knype FC – a thinly disguised Stoke – and includes a long and lyrical description of the archaic system of relaying football results by pigeon post.

In his novel *The Card* (1911) – which labels football 'the one ancient and glorious sport which appeals to the reason and heart of England' – Bennett articulates through his character Denry Machin a knowing maxim. When asked by his wife 'what football has got to do with being mayor' he sagely informs her that 'football has got to do with everything.'

In *Things That Have Interested Me* (1923–26) Bennett cited association football as a consistent thread in his life. Although born in the same town as the famous Stoke City player Stanley Matthews he also took pains to acknowledge Port Vale in his works under the guise of Bursley FC. Scholars have been unable to divine which of the two Potteries clubs claimed his greater allegiance.

Bennett's death in London resulted from typhoid fever contracted in Paris, where he defiantly drank a glass of water in a hotel dining room despite being warned it was unsafe. His ashes are buried in Burslem Cemetery in the Potteries.

BENNETT, WALTER, an outside-right twice capped by England (1901–02) while at Sheffield United, lost his life in ironic circumstances on April 6, 1908. Born in 1874 in Mexborough, Yorkshire, he became a miner, but escaped the horrors of the pit for the safer haven of football. Blessed with one of the hardest shots in the game, he was said to have scored 80 goals in a single season for Mexborough Town.

After winning 1898 League Championship and 1899 FA Cup winners' medals with Sheffield United he joined Bristol City. But when his career at Ashton Gate ended in 1907 he returned to Yorkshire and to the mining industry whence he had blessedly escaped. A year later, when a pit roof caved in at Denaby Main Colliery, 'Cocky' Bennett was one of the fatalities.

BENSON, ROBERT WILLIAM, the Woolwich Arsenal and England full-back born at Whitehaven, Cumbria, on February 9, 1883, died on February 19, 1916, after his comeback game ended in tragedy. He made his name at Sheffield United (1905–13), where in 273 League appearances he scored 20 goals. He was known for an unusual penalty-taking routine – a colleague would place the ball while Benson ran all the way from his defensive position to strike it.

In 1913 Bob Benson joined Arsenal, but when World War One began he took work at the munitions factory which gave the club its name. Having forsaken the game almost completely he returned to Highbury to watch a wartime match between his old team-mates and Reading. When it transpired Arsenal were a man short, Benson was persuaded to leave the stand to pull on a shirt for his 54th appearance. In his first outing in over a year the pace troubled him, and during the second half he had to leave the field dizzy with exertion. He died in the Highbury dressing room soon afterwards and was laid to rest in his Arsenal shirt, aged only 33.

BERNERS, DAME JULIANA, born *circa* 1388, is described in historical texts as a Benedictine nun who was Prioress of Sopwell Nunnery near St Albans, Hertfordshire. She died at a date unknown, although she was recorded 'still living' in 1460. Her obituary is sealed via an iconic lexical moment, for by her own fair hand the word 'football' (in its rudimentary spelling) was first written in 'English proper'. Earlier allusions to the pastime were recorded in Latin, French or Anglo-Scots.

Her seminal use of a word now globally recognised survives in a later printed transcript, the 1486 edition of the *Boke of St Albans*, which carries her name as author. In a section describing types of ball she says: 'The term *pila* in Latyn is taken for a certain rounde instrument to play with. While to the hande it is calde *pila manualis*, and other while it is an instrument for the foote and is then calde *pila pedalis*, a *fote bal*.'

John Bale's *Lives of the Most Eminent Writers of Great Britain* (1559) said of Berners that 'amongst the many solaces of human life she held the sports of the field in the highest estimation.' As such, she was also the author of *A Treatyse of Fysshynge with an Angle*, and has been much romanticised by rod and line enthusiasts. However, her life and very existence remain shrouded in mystery.

Some historians suggest her title was the *nom de plume* of a publicity-shy male. Yet the British Library records her name and holds an engraved likeness. Camps remain split, but those who espouse her cause have posed a not unreasonable rhetorical question: 'Who in medieval England would have mustered the imagination to invent a sporting nun, and if so why?'

BETTS, MORTON PETO, also known as 'A.H. Chequer', was the pseudonymous scorer of the first goal in an English FA Cup Final. Born at 29 Tavistock Square, Bloomsbury, London, on August 30, 1847, he died in France, on April 19, 1914, aged 66. Formerly of Harrow Chequers he played principally for the Wanderers, achieving his notable feat on March 16, 1872, when they beat Royal Engineers 1–0 at the Kennington Oval in the first ever final of the English Cup. *The Field* elucidated: 'A quarter of an hour had elapsed when R.W.S. Vidal middled the ball so cleverly to "A.H. Chequer" that the latter was able to effect the reduction of the military goal with but little difficulty' – Betts's quaint pseudonym stood for 'a Harrow Chequer', an oblique nod to his former side who had obligingly scratched when drawn against Wanderers in an early round.

The Football Annual praised Betts as 'a most effective dribbler, an invaluable man in any position' – in his one appearance for England (a 3–1 defeat by Scotland in 1877) he was goalkeeper. He also played three first-class cricket matches – for Middlesex (1872) and Kent (1872 and 1881) – and was secretary of Essex County Cricket Club (1887–90). For 20 years he sat on the FA Council and by profession was a civil engineer. He resided for some years in South America and Denmark, but met his end at his retirement abode 'Villa Massa' near Menton, on the Côte d'Azur.

BIRKETT, REGINALD HALSEY, who died in Wimbledon on June 30, 1898, was the first man to represent England at both association and rugby football. When he kept goal for Clapham Rovers in their 1880 FA Cup Final win, Birkett had already played four times for his country at rugby union and once at soccer. He shares the feat with only two other men – C.P. Wilson and J.W. Sutcliffe.

Educated at Lancing College, he was a member of the original committee of the Rugby Football Union in 1871, while his brother L. Birkett and his son J.G.G. Birkett were also England rugby internationals. At football he was considered 'a most reliable goalkeeper who knows how to use his hands but is apt to run out too much.' Born in Bishopsgate, London, on March 28, 1849, he was by profession a hide and skin broker in the City. His untimely death aged 49 followed an accident sustained while suffering from delirium during an attack of typhoid fever.

BLOOMER, STEPHEN, football's first 'household name', died in Derby, aged 64, on April 16, 1938. Born in Cradley, in the Black Country, on January 20, 1874, he became the foremost professional striker of the Victorian age. His prolific scoring record during the 1890s earned him the informal title 'the best footballer in the world'. His 28 England goals were gained in only 23 games (1894–1905) and he scored in each of his first ten internationals. For Derby County and Middlesbrough between 1892 and 1914 he garnered 394 goals in 655 games.

In 1914 he went to coach in Germany and was detained in a civilian prison camp throughout World War One. When manager of the Spanish side Real Irun (1923–25) he twice inflicted sensational home defeats on Real Madrid – 3–0 and 7–0 – and created further shock waves by leading his team of Basque amateurs to unlikely victory in the Copa del Rey. The Irun fans dubbed him 'Saint Stephen'.

No player had more sobriquets – 'Paleface', the 'Twisting Tormentor', the 'Ghost in Boots', 'Destroying Angel', 'Hammer of the Scots' and simply 'Steve'. *Association Football and the Men Who Made It* (1906) labelled him 'as crafty as an oriental' and 'slippery as an eel'. His sickly complexion and a feigned indifference when not on the ball belied a sinewy strength, raw pace and canny alertness, which with speed of thought and rapid shooting made him lethal at the crucial moment.

His final days were tinged with irony. In failing health he was dispatched on a luxury recuperative cruise paid for by Derby County, but died three weeks after his return, at his daughter's public house, the Great Northern Inn, where he had lived his last few years.

BOWEN, EDWARD ERNEST, a clergyman's son, born in Wicklow, Ireland, on March 30, 1836, died at Moux, near Dijon, France, on April 8, 1901. A half-back, he played for Wanderers in the first FA Cup Final (1872) and gained a winner's medal at the veteran age of 35 years and 352 days, an achievement he replicated the following season when a year older still.

His sporting ambition extended to cricket – he was a member

of M.C.C. and in his only first-class match, for Hampshire in 1864, failed to trouble the scorer in either innings – and he excelled at rowing, athletics, shooting, skating, cycling and mountaineering. He was a noted pedestrian who, when an undergraduate at Trinity College, Cambridge, walked the 90 miles to Oxford in 26 hours.

From 1859 until his death Bowen was senior assistant master at Harrow School, where he wrote the school song 'Forty Years On', which appeared in his *Harrow Songs and Other Verses*. Considering his athleticism the manner of Bowen's passing was unfortunate. On a cycling holiday on the Continent he fell in attempting to mount his machine and died almost instantly, aged 65. His body was brought back to Harrow for burial.

BRODIE, CHARLES THOMAS GEORGE, an accident-prone Scottish goalkeeper, died aged 63 in April 2000, having been labelled by the *Sun* 'a walking mishap'. Playing for Brentford against Millwall in November 1965 he found a hand grenade which had been tossed into his net – after the pitch was evacuated the device proved not to be live. In a game at Lincoln City he was floored by the crossbar when his entire goal collapsed around him. His most celebrated misfortune occurred in the Brentford v. Colchester game in November 1970 – while gathering a harmless back pass his knee was shattered in a collision with a stray dog. The bizarre accident ended his first-class career.

Even then his distinctive brand of bad luck persisted – playing for non-League Margate in November 1971 he was on the wrong end of an 11–0 defeat by Bournemouth in the FA Cup, and three months later broke an ankle. Nor did life beyond the game prove any less eventful – when working as a taxi driver in London he collided with a white Jaguar being driven by the England striker Geoff Hurst. 'Chic' Brodie was born in Duntocher, Scotland, on February 22, 1937, and played 402 League games for five clubs (1957–70).

BRODIE, JOHN ALEXANDER, city engineer for Liverpool (1898–1926), died aged 76 in 1934, the year that saw the fruition of the Mersey road tunnel project which he had embraced with vitality when it seemed but a distant possibility. His initiatives had a lasting impact far and wide – he proposed the building of the East Lancashire Road, was a pioneer of pre-fabricated housing, and became an expert in the field of town planning. To that end he was invited in 1912 to help with the site selection and design of the new capital of India – when New Delhi was finally declared open in 1931, Brodie was a guest of the Viceroy at the official ceremony.

Such grand designs aside, he counted a workaday contribution to football his proudest achievement. Aware as a sportsman of the perennial difficulty in the game's formative years of judging whether or not a ball had fairly bisected the goalposts, Brodie's sense of fair play led him to resolve to banish the problem for all time.

After sketching a design in barely 20 minutes he patented his invention in 1890 – 'a huge pocket into which the ball goes when a goal is scored' – and shrewdly negotiated a contract with the Football Association to supply his 'goal nets' at £3 12 shillings and sixpence a pair. After nets were first used in Football League games in 1891 the enduring principle was soon adopted worldwide.

In 2000 – along with former Beatle John Lennon (q.v.) – John Alexander Brodie was honoured by the City of Liverpool's inaugural 'Blue Plaque' scheme, his well-earned roundel adorning the large Victorian villa at 28 Ullet Road which had been his residence – Brodie Avenue in the city is also named in his honour. It is commonly held that the man first afforded the opportunity to ejaculate 'Back of the net!' was Fred Geary of Everton in 1891, who is thought to be the first player to have 'netted' in a recognised fixture.

BUDGERIGAR, PETER (THE), who died on April 3, 1996, seconds before the final whistle of the English Premier League game at Anfield between Liverpool and Newcastle United, became the subject of an acrimonious correspondence between his owner Dominic Hourd (an ardent fan of the Magpies) and the Liverpool striker Stan Collymore.

The supporter wrote to Collymore after he scored the injury-time winner in Liverpool's 4–3 victory, causing Hourd and his friend Peter Phillips, watching the game on Sky television, accidentally to knock the bird's cage off its stand in their ensuing frustration, thereby causing Peter's demise. The game was later voted 'Match of the Decade' and the result helped fatally erode what had been a 12-point lead at the top of the Premiership for Kevin Keegan's Newcastle.

Hourd accused Collymore of "'budgiecide" by remote means', later saying: 'He can't bring Peter the Budgie back now, but I told him I will never forgive him for what he did.' As Peter fell, commentator Martin Tyler unwittingly marked the tragic occasion: 'Kevin Keegan hangs his head – he's devastated.'

BULL, NAPOLEON (THE), was tragically put down at the age of four in February 2000 after slipping and breaking a leg whilst performing mating duties on a heifer. The magnificent one-ton pedigree beast, the father of over 200 calves, was the much-revered mascot of Hereford United Football Club, his live appearances generally confined to important games or cup ties when he would be paraded around the pitch perimeter suitably fettered. A jocular suggestion that the bull should be eaten at a celebration dinner was described by a club official as 'in the worst possible taste'. A supporters' club spokesperson asked to comment on Napoleon's sorry end said, 'It's a hell of a way to go.'

BUNYAN, CHARLES, accorded the debatable epithet 'the world's worst goalkeeper', died on August 3, 1922, at Ixelles, Belgium, aged 53. Between 1884 and 1908 he patrolled the line with mixed success for over a dozen clubs, Derby County and Sheffield United the most senior. His career developed along haphazard lines and among many encounters he may have wished to erase from memory was a Division Two game at Darwen on Boxing Day 1896 – guarding goal for Walsall (they played with only eight men), he was beaten 12 times without reply.

But his nadir had already occurred on October 15, 1887, in a first-round FA Cup tie at Preston North End. Bunyan was the beleaguered Hyde custodian whose posts were breached at the remarkable rate of once every 3 minutes 28 seconds – the 26–0 margin remains the highest for a competitive game in England. Even so, one observer wrote that he 'performed splendidly' and Bunyan disarmingly expressed the opinion that 'it might have been 40 had I not made so many good saves.'

He later exported his talents abroad – in 1910 being appointed cricket and football coach to Racing Club Brussels, one of the first Englishmen to manage overseas.

As a member of the Swedish Olympic Council he helped organise the 1912 Stockholm Games and in 1914 assumed charge of Belgium's national side, only for hostilities to precipitate his flight from Europe disguised as a Belgian refugee. Despite being above fighting age he returned to the front – with his sons Maurice and Ernie – as Lance Corporal Charlie Bunyan of the 'Footballers' Battalion' of the Middlesex Regiment.

Nicknamed 'Pilgrim's Progress' by team-mates, Bunyan will be remembered as an endearing if rather eccentric character. Whilst landlord of The Marquis of Hartington pub when a player at Chesterfield Town, he developed a lucrative sideline selling home-made shin guards alongside his beer. He was finally let go by the club's agitated board after one too many irresponsible forays into attack. He was born in Campton, Bedfordshire, in 1869, the illegitimate son of a straw plaiter in the hat trade, and his premature passing occurred whilst fulfilling yet another coaching assignment in his adopted Belgium.

BURGESS, NESTA, had been associated with Manchester United for over half a century when she died aged 92. She was considered a valued cog in the club's success, and at her funeral on March 9, 2007, manager Alex Ferguson and his entire first-team squad were present. Mrs Burgess was a native of Blaenau Ffestiniog, North Wales, and in her early years could speak only Welsh. She began working at Old Trafford in 1951, and in 1999 earned a UEFA award for services to football. She was the club's tea lady and general domestic, once earning 3d for each sock she darned. When she retired from full-time brewing she had served seven managers and a myriad of famous players.

CALLENDER, WILLIAM, the popular goalkeeper of Crystal Palace
Football Club, took his own life aged 29 in July 1932. The tall and
agile figure played 225 games from 1923 until his death, and had
become a greatly admired figure. Born in Prudhoe near Newcastle
on January 5, 1903, the circumstances of his end are unmatched in
football history for dramatic effect.

After his polio-stricken wife Eva passed away in May 1932,
the previously cheerful custodian became increasingly melancholic.
Two months after her death he was found hanging from a beam in
the Old Stand at Selhurst Park following a pre-season training session. No other player is known to have died by his own hand
whilst on club premises. Callender is also one of only a handful to
have allegedly revisited their former clubs in ghostly form, the
story being recounted in verse in *The Ghost of Selhurst Park*. The oft-
related embellishment that Billy Callender 'hanged himself from
his own crossbar' is merely sensational.

CAMSELL, GEORGE HENRY, a coal-miner turned England centre-forward, died aged 63 on March 7, 1966. With Second Division
Middlesbrough in 1926–27 he established an astonishing record of
59 League goals in 37 games, including nine hat-tricks. Lasting
supremacy would have been his had Everton's William Ralph
'Dixie' Dean not scored 60 First Division goals the very next
season.

Camsell was born in the pit village of Framwellgate Moor, near
Durham, on November 27, 1902. After beginning his League
career with Durham City in the Third Division North he signed
for Middlesbrough in 1925. He retired in 1939 the club's all-time

record scorer with 345 goals in 453 games. He scored in every one of his nine England appearances (1929–36), his 18-goal haul giving him a two-a-game strike-rate which no England player has bettered.

He later served Middlesbrough as coach, chief scout and secretary before retiring in December 1963. Although revered in Middlesbrough his name is little recognised in the football world at large, an astonishing oversight given his record. A career total of 345 League goals places George Camsell fifth in the Football League scorer rankings – only Arthur Rowley (q.v.), Dixie Dean, Jimmy Greaves and Steve Bloomer (q.v.) performed better.

CAMUS, ALBERT, the author and philosopher, born in Mondovi, Algeria, on November 7, 1913, died on January 4, 1960, in the French town of Villeblevin, where a monument stands in his memory. In the year he was awarded the Nobel Prize for literature (1957) he wrote in *France Football* of his consuming passion for goalkeeping. More recently his name has gained widespread currency in football's popular culture, although the majority of fans know little of his work.

He first became a goalkeeper at school – 'we were very poor and it wore out the shoes less quickly' – and in his teens played for Montpensier Sports Club. As an undergraduate (1933–36) he kept goal for Algiers University, but his declared ambition to play professionally was precluded by recurrent bouts of tuberculosis.

His football quotes were sometimes abstruse: 'What I most surely know about morality and the obligations of men, I owe to football.' A less well-aired example is more transparent: 'I quickly learned that the ball never behaves exactly as you expect it. This helped me in life, especially in France, where nobody plays it straight.'

Most supporters would find resonance in his rationale as a player: 'I loved my team so much, not only for the joy of victory, but also for the stupid desire to cry on evenings when we had lost.' As a fan he was both a purist and droll: 'My favourite team was Racing Club de Paris, who play scientifically, and quite often lose scientifically too, especially in matches they should win.'

He named his least favourite opponent as a centre-forward called Boufarik – nicknamed 'Watermelon' – who 'always got me in the kidneys, or put his knee in my distinguished parts'. He died aged 46 in a car accident, a fate he had once nominated 'the most absurd exit from life it is possible to imagine'.

CARR, JAMES LLOYD, the novelist, publisher, teacher, sporting romantic and celebrated English eccentric, who was born at Carlton Miniott, North Yorkshire, on May 20, 1912, died in his adopted Kettering, Northamptonshire, on February 26, 1994, aged 81. His critically acclaimed novel *A Month in the Country* was nominated for the 1980 Booker Prize.

Carr's fleeting success in the 1930s as an amateur footballer with South Milford White Rose inspired his literary legacy to the game. His 1975 novel *How Steeple Sinderby Wanderers Won the FA Cup* – in 2005 ranked 16th in the *Guardian*'s 'Top 50 Sports Books' – was described by the writer and football aficionado D.J. Taylor as 'a dazzling version of the time-honoured fantasy in which a village side goes on an unfettered rampage of giant-killing'.

Critics consider the whimsical tale the first to have distilled football's elusive essence – two full decades before Nick Hornby's *Fever Pitch* was similarly credited. Moreover, Carr's novel is said to be more lyrical. In the book, the stimulus for Wanderers' amazing achievement is the displaced Hungarian academic Dr Johannitsa Kossuth, who by scientific study derives seven postulations for certain success. Consequently it has been mooted only part in jest that no football club should appoint a manager without first seeking assurances that he will acquaint himself with Carr's masterpiece.

The book reflects the author's quirky character – when a headmaster he organised 'mathematics races' at school sports days, and in his garden displayed statues adorned with mirrors, set at such an angle that the sun would always shine through the windows of his house on his birthday.

J.L. Carr was survived by his gloriously unlikely plot. After defeating Aston Villa in a semi-final – staged incongruously at Wolverhampton – Sinderby lift the 'English Cup' after a 1–0 win at Wembley against Glasgow Rangers! The decisive goal is scored in the dying seconds by Alex Slingsby, after Sinderby have been kept in the game by their injured goalkeeper Alf 'Monkey' Tonks, playing his final match. The heroic custodian is by day a milkman, who on the back of the victory marries his sweetheart Maisie Twemlow, whose libido was legendary.

CATTERICK, HARRY, born in Darlington on November 26, 1919, was one of the greatest managers of the post-war years, reaching the pinnacle of his success with Everton in the 1960s and '70s. He died aged 65 on March 9, 1985. In the 1940s and early 1950s he was an Everton centre-forward – scoring 24 goals in 71 matches – and afterwards played for Crewe Alexandra. He achieved more as a manager, leading Everton to two League Championship titles and an FA Cup win. He retired from football in 1977 having latterly managed Preston North End.

He shares with the prolific scorer Dixie Dean a poignantly macabre passing, for both Everton legends died at the club's ground. Catterick suffered a fatal heart attack after watching Everton play Ipswich Town in an FA Cup quarter-final at Goodison Park. He was said to be stern but fair – dubbed 'the silent gentleman of football' – and a strict disciplinarian. One notable quirk was a fierce objection to players getting married during the season, as he believed that for several months afterwards they lost a yard of pace.

CATTON, JAMES ALFRED HENRY, known in the game as J.A.H.
'Jimmy' Catton, died at the age of 76 in 1936, already christened
'The Father of Football Journalism'. Born in Greenwich on April
6, 1860, he attended Malvern College, and on leaving became an
apprentice journalist with the *Preston Chronicle*. In 1886 he began
covering football for the famous sports paper *Athletic News* – first as
'Ubique' then 'Tityrus' – later becoming its long-reigning editor
until 1924.

Although diminutive in stature (being barely five feet tall), his
journalistic clout made him a giant of the game since *Athletic News*
was devoured feverishly by the fans and also served as a semi-offi-
cial mouthpiece for football's governing bodies. Thus were
reputations enhanced and ruined, causes advanced or rejected,
teams perhaps even picked, by a few finely crafted words from the
pen of 'Tityrus'.

Of his several sporting books, *Wickets and Goals* (1926) was the
most successful, much established wisdom concerning early football being derived from its pages. His turn of phrase was
economical but evocative – Preston's ranks boasted Jack Gordon 'a
human springbok', John Goodall 'as quiet as an old sheep', and
Nick Ross 'the demon back' who 'had teeth which were almost
green which he hissed through as he played'. Teams too were
summed up pithily – when they lost the 1915 Cup Final to
Sheffield United he wrote that 'Chelsea were as helpless as a reed
shaken in the wind.'

A genuine feeling for the game was substantiated by his lyrical
prose and dry wit, which never left him. He wrote that 'one likes to
administer the pill with a sugar coating', and not long before his
death – when 'old, tired, bald and grey' – informed his readers that
'my scanty locks are silvered o'er with the toll of years'. By the same
token it is impossible to suggest that football's first incurable romantic 'died' or even 'suffered death' – to quote a phrase of his own he 'was
summoned to that eternal greensward where play never ends'.

CAUNCE, LEWIS 'LEN', a goalkeeper who from 1932 to 1939 played 155 League games for Rochdale and Oldham Athletic, died aged 67 in 1978. Born in Earlestown, Lancashire, on April 20, 1911, he was in goal for Oldham when they were beaten 13–4 at Tranmere Rovers in a Third Division North game on Boxing Day 1935. It remains the highest aggregate score for a Football League match, and no keeper has let in more goals in a League game. Oldham devotees were quick to advance festive 'over-indulgence' as a possible cause, since when the two teams had met at Boundary Park only 24 hours earlier on Christmas Day, Tranmere had been comfortably beaten by four goals to one. Len Caunce's thoughts on the debacle were buried with him.

CHARLTON, ELIZABETH 'CISSIE', football's most celebrated and redoubtable matriarch, died on March 26, 1996. She was born Elizabeth Milburn on November 11, 1912, in Ashington, Northumberland, into a remarkable football clan. Four of her brothers played professionally – three with Leeds United – and her cousin John Milburn was the Newcastle United centre-forward of the fifties, the famous 'Wor Jackie'.

Elizabeth married a miner and had four sons – John, Robert, Gordon and Tommy – two of whom, better known as Jack and Bobby, achieved great fame in football. Both won World Cup medals with England in 1966. It was Cissie who personally coached the boys in their early years and nurtured them towards the professional game. Sadly she also became embroiled in an acrimonious split between the two Charlton brothers which became public after her death. 'Family differences' (she did not approve of his wife Norma) led to her favourite son Bobby all but spurning his mother towards the end of her life – Jackie commented after the funeral: 'I'll never forgive him. We've never been further apart than we are now. I just don't want to know him.'

She was the first female subject of a football biography – *Cissie: Football's Most Famous Mother* (1988) – was named 'Northern Personality of the Year' by the Variety Club, and was the first person to receive a 'Hearts of Gold' award from television's Esther Rantzen, a singular honour given to 'members of the public performing unsung acts of outstanding dedication or kindness'. Her granddaughter Suzanne Charlton also achieved a measure of celebrity as a television weather forecaster. 'Cissie' Charlton died in the town of her birth, aged 83.

CLEMENT, DAVID THOMAS, capped five times by England at right-back, was born in Battersea on February 2, 1948, and died on March 31, 1982. Aged only 34 he was still on the books of Wimbledon when he committed suicide, one of the few England internationals to do so. He came to prominence with his first club Queen's Park Rangers at a time when their ranks included Stan Bowles, Rodney Marsh and Gerry Francis. After 472 appearances (1966–79) he joined Bolton Wanderers and then Fulham. At his final club Wimbledon, a badly broken leg left him severely depressed when he believed his career was finished. Whilst recuperating he took his own life by poisoning himself with weed-killer. Dave Clement was survived by his wife and a three-year-old son Neil, who in 1996–97 made his own Football League debut with Chelsea, and subsequently played over 250 times for West Bromwich Albion.

COLMAN, DONALD CAMERON, died aged 66 on October 5, 1942. In addition to 'poise, pluck and shrewdness' the Scottish international full-back was said to have had 'an artistic streak' and a number of curiosities attach to his name.

He was born Donald Cunningham in Renton, Dunbartonshire, on August 14, 1878, but adopted his thinly disguised pseudonym (Colman was the surname of his grandmother) in a doomed attempt to conceal his football activities from a disapproving father.

His first-class career began with Motherwell in 1905 at the late age of 27, but his reputation was made in 349 games for Aberdeen, where he became the club's first 'true great'. Having begun with non-League Tontine Athletic (1895–96) and played until the age of 44 with Dumbarton (1922–23) his 27-season career was at that time considered a remarkable feat of endurance.

In 1931 he became Aberdeen's coach and is credited in that role with the 'invention' of the dugout. 'Introduced to British football' would better serve, as the so-called innovation had long been a feature of both American baseball and of football in Norway, where Colman had coached in the 1920s. A devotion to boxing and dancing gave him a particular appreciation of the importance of footwork – so to better study that of his players he had a pit excavated at Aberdeen's Pittodrie enclosure from where he scrutinised the game at ground level. The addition of a roof enabled Colman to keep his notebook dry – thus was the dugout born in Scotland.

Soon after playing a friendly in Aberdeen the same idea was introduced to England by Everton. The primitive device has latterly assumed iconic status in world football culture as 'the bench', reaching its epitome in the photographic history *Dugouts* (2006) in which Donald Colman is given an honoured place.

COMMON, ALFRED, the England forward born at Sunderland on May 25, 1880, died aged 65 in Darlington on April 3, 1946, where he had for many years been a popular licensee. His professional career (1900–14) embraced Sunderland, Sheffield United, Middlesbrough, Arsenal and Preston North End, but his pivotal place in the game's annals is as the subject of the first four-figure transfer, when in February 1905 he moved from Sunderland to struggling Middlesbrough for what was then considered the 'shocking' fee of £1,000. One affronted journalist called it 'flesh and blood for sale' and Parliament asked 'Where will it all end?' But more pragmatic observers pronounced Alf Common 'worth every penny' after his goals helped 'Boro narrowly avoid relegation to the Second Division.

Only 5ft 8in but a hefty 13 stone he was described as 'a constant menace to opposing defences, powerful and aggressive in style, but off the field a jovial, humorous character'. He won three England caps (1904–06) and a 1902 FA Cup winner's medal with Sheffield United, his career record being 124 goals in 388 League games. Transfer fees spiralled after Common's move and the year after his death a new landmark was reached when Tommy Lawton was sold by Chelsea to Notts County for the gargantuan sum of £20,000.

CONLIN, JAMES, the archetypal 'diminutive winger', was killed aged 35 in Flanders on June 23, 1917, while serving with the 15th Highland Light Infantry. Born in Consett, County Durham, on July 6, 1881, it was said that 'a more colourful character would be hard to find'. Hibernian, Falkirk and Albion Rovers all benefited from his 'tricky wing skills and pinpoint centres' before at Bradford City (1904–06) he became both the club's first international (with one England cap) and the first City player to be sent off.

His £1,000 move to Manchester City was only the second four-figure transfer, and on his City debut at Arsenal on September 1, 1906, he became the first player to appear in a Football League game with a knotted handkerchief on his head. Played in unseasonable heat the game proved farcical. Several City debutants expressed themselves unable to cope with the scorching sunshine – two retired at half-time and in the second half City were reduced to five fit men. Jimmy Conlin himself had left the field but gamely rejoined the action before a better adapted Arsenal graciously settled for a 4–1 win.

After a spell with Birmingham City he ended his career at Airdrie in 1913 after admitting a serious drink problem. Conlin played 243 Football League games, scored 35 goals, and has no known grave.

CONNOR, JAMES, who in 1886 played his only game for Scotland – as goalkeeper in a 7–2 defeat of Ireland – died on January 29, 1899, aged only 37. A founder member of Airdrieonians in 1878 (known then as Excelsior) he filled both goal and occasional outfield berths, and in the 1890s was briefly club secretary.

Yet his life would occasion no lasting interest but for the unique distinction which befell Connor at Broomfield Park during Airdrie's home game against Royal Albert on June 6, 1891. On that day he became the first goalkeeper in the world to face a penalty kick in a recognised game, the new rule having been approved by the Scottish FA only a few days earlier.

Even so, that same body then cast dubiety on Connor's place in history by swiftly decreeing that the kick had been 'illegally awarded' by an over-zealous official, since the 'rule' was not scheduled to become 'law' until September 1891.

Connor was born in Airdrie on February 22, 1861, and was his home town club's first internationalist.

COOK, THOMAS EDWIN REED, a centre-forward, the first Brighton and Hove Albion player capped by England (1925), and the club's record scorer – 114 goals in 190 League games (1922–29) – took a fatal overdose of tablets on January 15, 1950, aged 48. Latterly dogged by ill health he had also been haunted by wartime memories of his escape from an aircraft in which all his fellow crew members burnt to death. Born at Cuckfield, Sussex, on February 5, 1901, Tommy Cook was also a Sussex county cricketer – over 20,000 runs and 80 wickets – and was once nominated 'Sussex's finest sportsman'. A bus in the Brighton and Hove fleet (number

623) is named after him, an honour also bestowed on the sports broadcaster Desmond Lynam (no longer in service), a former Brighton and Hove Albion director.

COWAN, SAMUEL, whose 407 games for Manchester City (1924–35) were supplemented by three caps for England, died at Haywards Heath, West Sussex, on October 4, 1964. The former centre-half collapsed from a heart attack whilst officiating at a benefit match for the Sussex county cricketer Jim Parks, and died in the dressing room soon afterwards, aged 63. Cowan had been the masseur to both Sussex and M.C.C., also to Brighton Ice Hockey Club.

He captained Manchester City to three FA Cup Finals – in 1933 after his second defeat Cowan vowed to the Duke of York as he was presented with a loser's medal that he would return to Wembley the next year to lift the trophy. The pledge was duly kept when City beat Portsmouth 2–1 in 1934. Born in Chesterfield, Derbyshire, on May 10, 1901, Sam Cowan is thought to be the only professional player to have died whilst refereeing a football match.

CRAIG, ALBERT, 'The Surrey Poet', whose larger-then-life presence graced many a football and cricket match, died at 8 Mayflower Road, Clapham, on July 8, 1909, in his 60th year. Born in Yorkshire in 1849, and brought up there, he began work as a Post Office clerk in Huddersfield, but on discovering a peculiar talent for verse-making dedicated himself to celebrating the deeds of footballers and cricketers in humorous rhyme. These the self-styled 'captain of the crowd' sold as broadsheets at matches.

His poetry was seldom of the highest order – it was recorded that 'he had no authority but popularity, no recommendation but gaiety, and no talent but wit' – yet he was welcomed without fail up and down the country, where his good-natured chaff and banter with the crowds enlivened many a dull encounter.

When he died after a protracted illness an admirer swiftly published *Cricket and Football: Rhymes, Sketches, Anecdotes of Albert Craig, the 'Surrey Poet'*. Yet Craig himself had no illusions about the quality of his work. When touting a masterpiece around a ground he would shout: 'I know that any fool among you could write a better poem than this, but I defy anyone else, however intelligent, to sell it at 2d a copy.'

CRESWELL, COL. EDMUND WILLIAM, a 'capital forward' with Royal Engineers, born in Gibraltar on November 7, 1849, died aged 81 at Copse Hill, Ewhurst, Surrey, on May 1, 1931. In the first FA Cup Final (1872) – Royal Engineers v. Wanderers – he established the long tradition of Cup Final heroism, when he doggedly continued despite breaking his collarbone early on. *The Sportsman* said: 'Too much praise cannot be accorded to him for the pluck he showed in maintaining his post – although completely disabled and in severe pain – until the finish.' Despite his game approach Wanderers prevailed 1–0. Creswell later played cricket for Hampshire (1889) before they were ranked first-class. His father was Gibraltar's chief postmaster.

CRIPPS, HENRY RICHARD 'HARRY', the Millwall left-back between 1961 and 1974, died aged 54 on December 29, 1995, having become a cult hero to the club's famously committed adherents. The tags 'hatchet man' and 'bone-crunching tackle' might have been invented for him – he was said to be the perpetrator of more broken legs than any other player in the history of the League. His reputation was such that it was not unknown for youngsters of later generations to believe that his grisly deeds and even his very being were entirely made up – his nicknames 'The Dog' and 'Arry Boy' scarcely reduced that possibility.

Born in East Dereham, Norfolk, on April 29, 1941, he made a record 447 appearances for Millwall and scored 40 goals, it being said of his stiffly brisk canters upfield that 'the forward motion gained in irresistibility what it lacked in speed'. He later became a coach and was briefly affiliated in a 'chalk and cheese' partnership at Southend United with the former England captain Bobby Moore.

Following his death from a heart attack his playing colleague Eamon Dunphy recalled: 'He was a gentle soul at heart,' while another team-mate Keith Weller said, 'He was a cheat but a nice one.' He was survived by a pungent keepsake – the *Independent* columnist Peter Corrigan wrote in 2004: 'My most prized souvenir is Harry Cripps's jockstrap, which carries his signature.'

CROMWELL, OLIVER, Lord Protector of the Commonwealth, died on September 3, 1658, from complications arising following a bout of European malaria. Born in Huntingdon on April 25, 1599, he is one of the few great historical figures whose participation in football is documented, and the first player to have named his 'most difficult opponent' in the time-honoured fashion.

James Heath's *Life, Death, Birth and Burial of Oliver Cromwell* (1663) said:

'When an undergraduate at Cambridge he was more famous for his exercises in the fields than in the schools – in which he never had the honour of a degree – being one of the chief match makers and players at football.'

The veracity of this was further corroborated in a letter written after Cromwell's death – dated January 3, 1708 – which refers to his Cambridge football adversary John Wheelwright, later a clergyman in Massachusetts: 'Cromwell could remember the time when he had been more afraid of meeting Wheelwright at football than of later meeting an army in the field, for he was infallibly sure of being tripped up by him.'

Cromwell's credentials for a lasting place in the game have on occasion been overstated. It has been erroneously said that the Cromwell Cup – football's second-oldest competition, won by

Sheffield Wednesday on February 15, 1868 – was named in his honour. Indeed it was named after Oliver Cromwell, but in this case the manager of the Theatre Royal in Sheffield, the competition sponsors.

CROPPER, ARTHUR, part of the Norwich City forward line in 23 League games from 1927 until 1929, died aged 43 on October 25, 1949. He ended his playing days with non-League Yarmouth Town, and it was in the Norfolk coastal resort that he engineered an unusual claim to fame – Cropper is one of few footballers whose image has adorned a pub sign, and he is thought to be the earliest such claimant by some margin.

When landlord of the town's incongruously named East Suffolk Tavern – it honoured the army's 12th Regiment of Foot, East Suffolk – Cropper was unable to resist capitalising on his minor celebrity and elected to depict his likeness on the hostelry's sign in the act of playing football.

Greater players since thus honoured include Arsenal's Charlie George, whose image adorned The Gunners public house close to Highbury Stadium, and Jackie Stamps, scorer of two goals for Derby County in their 1946 Cup Final triumph over Charlton Athletic, after whom a pub in Derby market place was transiently named. Arthur Cropper had a brother, Reginald, who played with him for Norwich City. Latterly the East Suffolk Tavern in South Town Road, Yarmouth, has continued to dispense 'wines, ales and spirits' and is popularly known as 'Cropper's Bar'.

CROSSE, KNYVETT, capped three times at half-back by Wales (1879–81), died in Liverpool aged 61 on November 19, 1916. Born in Pontesbury, Shropshire, in 1855, he is the only international to have played under a pseudonym expressly inspired by the name of a bookstall.

While with Druids and Ruabon he assumed the name K.

Smith – Crosse was manager of the W.H. Smith bookstall at Ruabon station – as he was anxious that his employers should not get to know of his secret life in football. For many years he captained Bangor Cricket Club and in retirement was proprietor of the Star Hotel in Bangor, having become sufficiently emboldened to use his own name over the door.

DAVIES, FREDERICK, the celebrated coracle maker, an unlikely hero of British football, died aged 83 in November 1994 in Shrewsbury, where for 45 years he had served the town's football club in unique fashion. During Shrewsbury Town home games he sat in his coracle afloat the River Severn dutifully anticipating the emergence of a stray football from within the bounds of the Gay Meadow enclosure. Once the inevitable occurred he and his rustic craft combined, retrieving the ball from the water to enable the game to proceed without loss. Having achieved notability on account of the service, he retired in 1986 a folk-hero. When Shrewsbury Town announced plans to leave Gay Meadow in 2007 for pastures new, one emotion-fuelled fan composed a tribute to 'The Coracle Man':

> When a ball met the river
> Fred Davies would shiver
> In his coracle boat
> The ball would be captured
> Supporters enraptured
> And the game stayed afloat.

Through his recovery acts Davies achieved the unlikely etymological feat of disseminating the word 'coracle' throughout the football world. For his trouble he earned between 25 pence and 50 pence per ball retrieved. His record haul in a single season was 130.

DIXON, JOHN AUGER, born in Grantham, Lincolnshire, on May 27, 1861 – a director of dressmakers Dixon and Parke Ltd – died at his home in The Park, Nottingham, on June 8, 1931, aged 70 years.

While a Notts County winger in the pre-League era he played once for England in a 1–1 draw against Wales in 1885.

In the same season he assisted the celebrated amateurs Corinthians – scoring twice in his only two games – before ill health precipitated his retirement from football. He is better known as a Nottinghamshire cricketer (1882–1905). Despite bagging a pair on his debut he later captained the county and scored 9,527 runs, including 13 centuries. As a bowler he took a hat-trick against Lancashire in 1887, although the easier football equivalent always eluded him.

In recognition of his 40 years' service on the Nottinghamshire committee the main entrance gates to Trent Bridge cricket ground were named after him. John Auger Dixon apart, no other dress-maker of note has played football for England.

DOG, NELL (THE), faithful watchdog to Manchester City FC, one of a small but elite number of canines to achieve a measure of celebrity in football circles, perished on the night of November 6, 1920, in distressing circumstances. The Airedale terrier was killed when the all-wooden Main Stand at City's Hyde Road ground was destroyed by fire. The cause was not, as might be surmised, a stray firework, but a cigarette end carelessly discarded after that afternoon's reserve match. Nell's death was not in vain – the conflagration precipitated City's move in 1923 to Maine Road, the famous enclosure in Moss Side at which they stayed until May 2003.

DOG, PICKLES (THE), whose eventful life ended on August 3, 1971, earned his enduring fame on Sunday March 27, 1966, when in Beulah Hill, Upper Norwood, London, he discovered wrapped in newspaper the World Cup which had been stolen seven days earlier while in the 'safe keeping' of the Football Association. The FA's bacon saved, England won the trophy at Wembley Stadium on July 30.

Pickles was given a medal by the National Canine Defence

League plus a year's supply of doggie treats and an acting role in the film *The Spy with the Cold Nose*. He enjoyed the celebrity life immensely but sadly died when strangled by his lead, which caught in a fallen tree while he was in merry pursuit of a cat.

DONEGAN, ANTHONY JAMES. 'Lonnie' Donegan, the 'King of Skiffle', considered Britain's first musical 'superstar', was born on April 29, 1931, and died on November 3, 2002. His football obituary is earned for his 1965 single release 'World Cup Willie'. Although initially a flop the record attained cult status after England beat Germany in the 1966 final. Since Donegan was born in Glasgow his talismanic contribution has been labelled by England fans 'deliciously ironic'.

Willie was the first World Cup mascot and the ditty the progenitor of an entire new industry in World Cup songs. While the lovable lion became synonymous with the England team he was also embraced by their rivals with some affection. When Scotland narrowly failed to qualify for the 1966 finals, the *Daily Express* depicted a kilted Willie in tears – arguably a sardonic joke. More incongruous still was the glorious own goal scored by the German players – England's final opponents had earlier recorded a German-language cover version – 'Fussball Willi' – which is now a collector's piece.

While it was Donegan who assured Willie's lasting celebrity, the man after whom he was named was Ken Willson, a chief organiser of the 1966 tournament. Stocky, with square shoulders and a pugnacious jaw, his habitual strutting of the FA corridors roaring orders was picked up on by the office girls. They dubbed him 'World Cup Willie' and when the drawings of the unnamed mascot were unveiled, the likeness to Willson was so uncanny that the christening ceremony formalised the epithet. Donegan's death occurred in Peterborough, in the midst of a tour, while still actively pursuing his career at the age of 71. He was survived by his wife and his lyrics:

Dressed in red, white and blue, that's World Cup Willie,
We all love him too, World Cup Willie,
He's tough as a lion, and never will give up,
That's why Willie . . . is favourite for the cup.

DOYLE, SIR ARTHUR CONAN, MD, the creator of Sherlock Holmes, born at Edinburgh on May 22, 1859, died at Crowborough, Sussex, on July 7, 1930, aged 71. From 1884 to 1890 – when a medical practitioner in Southsea, Hampshire – he played 79 games for Portsmouth AFC, the amateur side later dubbed 'the original Pompey'. Doyle was a leading light in running the club, playing both in goal and at full-back, often using the pseudonym A.C. Smith, and on occasion W. Smith. Having pioneered association football in the naval port, the club disbanded in 1896, and two years later the current Portsmouth FC was formed.

In *Memories and Adventures* (1924) Doyle wrote:

> I was always too slow to be a really good back, though I was a long and safe kick. After a long hiatus I took up football again in South Africa and organised a series of inter-hospital matches in Bloemfontein, which helped take our minds away from enteric. My old love treated me very scurvily, however, for I received a foul from a man's knee which buckled two of my ribs and bought my games to a close. I have played occasionally since, but there is no doubt that as a man grows older a brisk charge shakes him up as it never did before. Let him turn to golf, and be thankful that there is still one splendid game which can never desert him.

Sherlock Holmes evaded football with a vengeance, but in the rugby story *The Adventure of the Missing Three-Quarter* (1904) Doyle mischievously allows a dog named 'Pompey' to unlock the mystery.

It has been mooted that his description of the creature could well be a playful allusion to Doyle the erstwhile full-back: 'No very great flier, as his build will show, but a staunch hound on a scent.'

DRUMMOND, JOHN, capped 14 times by Scotland at full-back (1892–1903), died on January 24, 1935. He set out in 1886 with Falkirk, but accrued his true renown at Rangers (1892–1903), where with Nicol Smith he formed one of the greatest rearguard partnerships the club has known. A contemporary wrote: 'Drummond kicked with both feet and was fond of finding touch, but his style – so bounciful and brave – left him open to the want of recovery.'

Assiduous statisticians have bestowed upon Jock Drummond an unusual claim to fame. He was the last outfield player in first-class football to perform wearing a cap – said to have been 'to keep his head cool'. Born at Alva, Clackmannanshire, on April 13, 1870, he was 64 at his death. His ally in defence failed to survive him – Nicol Smith perished aged 31 in January 1905, after contracting enteric fever.

DUCAT, ANDREW, one of only 17 men in the twentieth century to play for England at both football and cricket, died aged 56 in St John's Wood, London, on July 23, 1942, when apparently in the full glow of health. Born in Brixton, London, on February 16, 1886, he played 188 games for Woolwich Arsenal and led Aston Villa when they beat Huddersfield Town in the 1920 FA Cup Final. His move to Fulham (1921) proved an unhappy one – in 1924 he became the first former Fulham player to manage the club, and in 1924 the first Fulham manager to be sacked. His six caps for England (1910–20) were won at half-back.

He made 23,733 runs for Surrey (1906–31) and played one Test for England. His 306 not out against Oxford University (1919) is the highest score by an active professional footballer in the first-class game. Ducat later became cricket coach at Eton College and was also an accomplished sports reporter.

He died with his boots on – cricket boots – the only man to perish whilst taking part in a match at Lord's Cricket Ground. Batting number five for Surrey Home Guard against Sussex Home Guard, he collapsed and died at the crease after lunch, a weak heart being blamed. The match was abandoned – although less respectfully it has been related with jocularity that the score-card read 'Private A. Ducat, not out 29, dead'.

He was survived by his wife and daughter and his non-striking batting partner Lieutenant R.H. Attwell, who said: 'I removed Andy's false teeth, gave his heart a thump and tried artificial respiration, but to no avail. His loved ones had gone shopping and when they returned to the ground to learn what had happened it was most distressing for them.' Attwell was 'not out 1' at the time of the tragedy.

DUNLOP, JAMES, who was born in Paisley, near Glasgow, on May 17, 1870, died there on January 11, 1892, his short but promising football career being ended in the cruellest fashion. As a youth Dunlop played with the junior side Underwood Strollers, graduating to Paisley's senior club St Mirren in 1888–89.

Such was his progress that on March 22, 1890, he made his Scotland debut in a 5–0 victory over Wales, which proved to be his sole cap. Tragedy befell the inside-left during St Mirren's New Year's Day friendly against Abercorn in 1892, when he fell on a piece of glass and sustained a cut which became infected. Ten days later, aged 22, he died of tetanus. Despite his tender years, Dunlop was known as 'Daddy' on account of his precocious talent for directing colleagues. Soon after his departure the people of Paisley erected a memorial in the town's Woodside Cemetery, which yet stands in his honour. He was the Paisley manager of the National Telephone Company.

EDELSTON, MAURICE, whose mellifluous radio commentaries defined a football epoch, was still broadcasting regularly when he died of a heart attack in Reading, on January 30, 1976, aged 57. Between 1967 and 1975 he covered every FA Cup Final and several dramatic Championship deciders – including Arsenal's win at Spurs in 1971 and Wolves' defeat of Leeds which handed Derby County the 1972 title.

Born in Hull on April 27, 1918, he was that rarity among commentators, an accomplished player. When only 18 he played for Great Britain at the 1936 Berlin Olympics and later made his name as an inside-forward with Reading – 202 League games and 70 goals 1946–51. He also played for Fulham, Brentford, and Northampton Town, and when still an amateur made five England wartime appearances in the company of ten professional team-mates.

His great friend the sports writer John Arlott (q.v.) labelled him 'the busiest player in the game, who never shrinks from the hefty traffic of close marking, and possesses that rare combination of a scholarly brain with extreme speed of mental reaction'. Edelston co-authored *Wickets, Tries and Goals* (1949) and *Masters of Soccer* (1960) and is thought unique among professional footballers in having a library named after him (at the Blue Coat School in Reading). His wing-half father Joe was the only player ever to be transferred on the high seas.

EDWARD II, H.M. KING, ruler of England between 1307 and 1327, died at Berkeley Castle, Gloucestershire, in September 1327, alleged to have been murdered in the vilest fashion. He was the first of many English monarchs to attempt without success to ban the playing of football, after the boisterous pastime had attained a pitch of popularity considered counter to the national good.

His royal proclamation in French was issued by the Lord Mayor of London Nicholas de Farndone on April 13, 1314:

> Forasmuch as there is great noise in the city caused by the rampaging pursuit of large footballs [*rageries de grosses pelotes de pee*] in the fields of the public from which many evils might arise which God forbid: we command and forbid on behalf of the King, on pain of imprisonment, such game to be used in the city in future.

Despite specimen prosecutions being duly brought, the popular diversion continued unabated. Between 1314 and 1667 football was officially banned in England by more than 30 royal and local laws, each without lasting effect.

The first monarch to have 'tried and failed' to quell what remains England's foremost sporting pastime was born in Caernarfon, Wales, on April 25, 1284, and his alleged murder in captivity aged 43 has been the subject of much debate. While generations of schoolboys have devoured the sensational version – that his internal organs were seared by a red-hot poker introduced through a horn sleeve inserted in his anus – historians believe the story to have been concocted.

EDWARDS, JOHN HAWLEY, was the founder and captain of Shropshire Wanderers (1873) and one of only two men to enjoy the unusual distinction of being capped at football for both England and Wales. His death aged 42 on January 14, 1893, at Old Colwyn, Denbighshire, followed a throat infection. Born at Pride Hill, Shrewsbury, on March 21, 1850, the *Shrewsbury Chronicle* said of his capabilities: 'Few forwards are better dribblers in this part of the country – his only fault is that he prefers a crooked course to a straight one.'

With Shropshire Wanderers in 1875 he reached the semi-final of the FA Cup and the following year won the trophy with the more celebrated Wanderers from Middlesex. His sole England cap was against Scotland (1874), who again provided the opposition when Edwards made his one appearance for Wales in their first ever international (1876). When the Welsh FA was formed in that year he became its first treasurer.

Educated at Shifnal Grammar School, and by profession a solicitor, Edwards was an able cricketer for both Shropshire and Warwickshire (not first-class) and in later life a keen angler. His celebrity knew few bounds – in 1889 he officiated as starter at the Shrewsbury Whit Monday Athletics Fête – and his lifelong support of the winter game in the county of his birth earned him a soubriquet of rare distinction – 'The Godfather of Shropshire Football'.

ELGAR, SIR EDWARD, the English composer of *Enigma Variations* (1899) and *Pomp and Circumstance* (1901), died on February 23, 1934, aged 76. Although born in the village of Lower Broadheath, Worcestershire, on June 2, 1857, he became a firm if somewhat 'fair-weather' adherent of Wolverhampton Wanderers, notably following their 1893 FA Cup Final triumph against Everton.

His interest was further aroused through his friend Reverend Alfred Penny, whose 21-year-old daughter Miss Dora subsequently accompanied the married composer, 17 years her senior, to games at Molineux. In *Memoirs of a Variation* (1937) she wrote of her first meeting with 'E.E.' on December 6, 1895: 'He didn't want to talk about music. He wanted to know if I ever saw the Wolverhampton Wanderers play – and when he heard that our house was close to the ground he became quite excited.'

Elgar's friendship – some sources have dared to suggest 'relationship' – with Dora, immortalised as 'Dorabella' in his tenth variation, was fictionalised by Keith Alldritt in *Elgar on the Journey to Hanley* (1979) in which the pair watch Wolves play Stoke. Dora later sent Elgar a press cutting praising his favourite player Billy Malpass – 'he banged the leather for goal' – the phrase so taking him that in 1898 he set it to music, a piece fancifully described by *The Times* a century later as 'the first football chant'. A tablet commemorating its 'author' was unveiled at Molineux in August 1998.

In true football tradition Elgar named his favourite meal as 'bangers and mash'. He was also a keen cyclist and nature lover – he had a bicycle named 'Mr Phoebus' and a rabbit called Peter. Sir Edward Elgar died in Worcester shortly after the discovery of a malignant tumour pressing on his sciatic nerve.

ESHAYA, YOURA, dubbed 'The Desert Footballer', who died aged 59 on July 21, 1992, in Sweden, where he had lived and coached for the preceding 20 years, attained widespread celebrity with an English Football League club without ever making a first-team appearance.

Born in Iran in 1933, his family moved to Iraq, and at 15 he captained the junior side of the RAF Assyrian Employees Club in Habbaniya, the desert outpost where his father was stationed. A skilful forward, barely five feet six inches tall, he was spotted by Flight Lieutenant R.K. Weston, a Bristol Rovers scout, and persuaded to join the club for the 1954–55 campaign. He was held back from first-team selection only by trivialities concerning a work permit.

Following a concerted campaign in support of his cause he was granted special dispensation by the Home Office to stay in Britain beyond his allotted time. He was found employment as a miner at Pensford Colliery, Somerset, but the lure of Iraq remained too strong. He returned there to take citizenship, starring for the Iraqi national side before his move to Scandinavia.

In his homeland he remains the revered subject of countless stories – in 1951, after playing and scoring against the Basra Select XI with a broken nose, he was voted 'most popular footballer in Habbaniya' by the *Iraq Times*. Their citation told how in his youth he had 'honed his heading ability by leaping to touch his mother's clothes line'.

Considered the first Iraqi attached to a British football club, the precise circumstances of his death are unique in football – he suffered a heart attack whilst conducting a training session with an Assyrian youth side in Gothenburg.

EVANS, ROBERT ERNEST, the Sheffield United stalwart once curiously tagged 'the best winger England and Wales ever had', died on November 28, 1965, at Chester, where he had been born in 1885. Between 1905 and 1908 he made his way modestly with Wrexham and Aston Villa, but after joining Sheffield United amassed 204 League appearances and 39 goals before a broken leg in 1919 ended his career.

Evans had appeared for Wales on ten occasions before the Sheffield United secretary John Nicholson tipped off the English FA in 1910 that the Blades' player had been born in Chester and had moved to Wales with his Welsh parents when barely three weeks old. The FA caused great controversy in Welsh football circles by objecting to his qualification, and Evans subsequently won four caps for England, including an appearance against Wales at Wrexham where four years earlier he had played for the Principality against England. John Hawley Edwards (q.v.) is the only other player to have represented both Wales and England in full internationals.

Described as 'unusually tall for a winger, covering the ground with a long, raking stride, and packing a stinging shot', Bobby

Evans was aged 80 years at his death, having four years earlier wit-
nessed the creation of the first '£100-a-week' footballer. That was
a stark contrast to his own start in the game, for on joining the
Welsh village club Bretton in 1900 when aged fifteen, Evans
meekly accepted in lieu of travelling expenses a weekly allowance of
two turnips.

EVERISS, FREDERICK, JP, born at Spon Lane, West Midlands, in 1882,
died aged 69 in 1951. His sobriquet 'Mr West Bromwich Albion' is
deserved. After joining the club in 1896, as a 14-year-old office
boy, he impressed the directors so much that in 1902 he was made
secretary-manager. He stayed in the post until 1948, his 46-year
stint making him the longest-serving manager in League football.
The average duration for the post is 2.97 years.

His successor as secretary was his son-in-law Ephraim Smith,
while Everiss became a director until his death. Even after his
passing, the dynasty continued, for his son Alan was Albion's secretary from 1960 until 1980, a family record of service to the club
which endured for a remarkable 84 years. By the time he died,
Fred Everiss had performed every role except player at Albion –
one of his jobs at The Hawthorns during the war years was ARP
nightwatchman.

FELSTEAD, ALBERT, a veteran of World War One, died in Podsmead Court care home at Gloucester, on July 22, 2001, aged 106. Born in Highgate, London, on October 28, 1894, he achieved unlikely late celebrity when the media discovered him to be the last surviving participant in the famous 'football truce' of 1915, when for the second and last year British and German soldiers broke off hostilities to briefly fraternise on Christmas Day.

His impromptu game took place between the freezing trenches near the village of Laventie in Northern France. He said: 'There was a bit of football if you could call it that – probably 50 or so a side and nobody kept score.' A fellow member of his regiment – the Royal Welch Fusiliers – was the writer Robert Graves, whose story *Christmas Truce* (1929) celebrated the football interlude. Graves had once been a keen player and is the surprise dedicatee in *The Boy's Book of Association Football* (1931) written by his brother John, a player with Casuals.

Bertie Felstead was demobbed in 1916 after being injured at the Battle of the Somme. He later worked for the General Electric Company. In his dotage he became 'an approachable Methuselah' and in an interview distilled the legend into a few sage words: 'I was an average man who experienced an extraordinary event. I took part because I loved football. The Germans were all right.'

FERGUSON, HUGH, the prolific marksman born in Motherwell on March 2, 1898, scorer of one of the most celebrated goals in football history, died in Dundee on January 9, 1930, at the young age of 31. Although never capped by Scotland, his 284 goals for Motherwell in ten seasons prompted a move in 1925 to Cardiff

City, with whom he registered his famous strike. In the 1927 Cup Final at Wembley he scored the solitary goal which enabled the trophy to leave England for the only time, the Welsh club's legendary triumph also causing the competition to be renamed from the 'English Cup' to the FA Cup.

Hughie Ferguson scored 77 League goals for Cardiff in four seasons before returning to Scotland in 1929 to play for Dundee, where the Dens Park faithful anticipated his scoring streak would continue. But when his former sharpness deserted him he was severely barracked and then dropped after struggling with injury, his Dundee record amounting to only 2 goals in 17 outings.

Despite the lame finish to his career Ferguson had lived every schoolboy's fantasy – a famous centre-forward who had scored the winning goal in a Wembley Cup Final – yet he was unable to cope when the glory days began to fade. Soon after losing his place in the Dundee side he gassed himself to death after attending a training session, leaving a wife and two children.

FLASHMAN, STANLEY, known as 'Fat Stan', the notorious ticket tout and spiv – although preferring to style himself a 'broker' – died aged 63 in Ilford in December 1999, after a battle against Alzheimer's disease. Born in the East End of London on December 3, 1936, the son of a tailor, he began by selling pots and pans in Houndsditch, but in the sixties graduated to the trade which earned him dubious fame and no little fortune, before a treacherous descent into bankruptcy.

Football was his forté – FA Cup Final tickets especially – but Flashman claimed an ability to secure entry to almost anything 'if the colour of the money is right' – Wimbledon tennis finals were a speciality, and he was even rumoured to have sold invitations for both a Royal garden party at Buckingham Palace and the wedding of Princess Anne.

Although operating from an insalubrious office in north

London, the trappings of gaudy wealth were conspicuously displayed at Flashman's mansion in Totteridge, near Barnet, which he shared with his wife Helen, who had been working as a nightclub hostess when they met – one football manager who visited their home remarked upon the 'wads of notes littered about the living room' while outside sat a Mercedes-Benz, registration 777 SF.

In 1985 Flashman made himself a hero with Barnet fans by paying £50,000 to save the non-League club from bankruptcy, and under his chairmanship in 1991 they miraculously achieved Football League status. But an abrasive style precipitated Flashman's spectacular downfall. Ignoring the protocol observed by most chairmen, he threatened supporters, assaulted television crews and attacked photographers – manager Barry Fry was repeatedly 'sacked' and reinstated, and Flashman once asked a female supporter: 'Do you want me to permanently mark your face?'

Football's original 'Mr Sleaze' resigned in 1993 due to ill health – shortly after the Inland Revenue had seized Barnet's books – leaving financial chaos in his gargantuan wake. Flashman was declared bankrupt and moved to the modest property in Ilford where he passed away. He was survived by a wife and sundry creditors, all of whom wondered where the money had gone.

Few in football mourned the passing of the 'Lord of the Black Market', only Barry Fry making a lame stab at a respectable epitaph: 'If you didn't know Stanley you would think he was an ignorant pig. Let's just say he was a Jekyll and Hyde character.'

FOOTBALL, THE RIGHT HONOURABLE GAME, which each Shrovetide since time immemorial had been riotously enjoyed in the Derbyshire town of Ashbourne, was heartlessly slain by Lord Cockburn on November 14, 1860, through powers vested in him by the 1837 Highways Act.

A case had been brought by local magistrates against Mr

George Woolley, a draper, whose pursuit of the revered leather through the streets of Ashbourne was said to have 'obstructed the passage of two carts'. On appeal to the highest legal authority Woolley was found guilty, and Ashbourne's chastened townsfolk pronounced the grave news by means of a satirical broadsheet:

> It becomes our painful duty to record the death of the Right Honourable game football, which melancholy event took place in the Court of Queen's Bench on Wednesday, November 14, 1860. For some months the patriotic Old Man had been suffering from injuries sustained in his native town and was removed by appeal to London, where he lingered in suspense till the law of death put its icy hand upon him. His untimely end has cast a gloom over the place, where the amusement he afforded the inhabitants will not soon be forgotten.

By great good fortune the deceased game was outlived by countless Ashburnians unwilling to accept its demise. With scant regard for the law, the rude and manly pastime was joyously resurrected the very next year, and subsequently received the patronage of the monarchy. The remarkable folk survival that is 'Ashbourne Royal Shrovetide Football' is still played in the town each year, and the longevity of the 'patriotic Old Man' was marked in 2007 by the feature documentary film *Wild in the Streets*.

FORD, TREVOR, the Welsh international centre-forward who played for Aston Villa, Cardiff City, Sunderland and Swansea Town, died aged 79 on May 29, 2003, after a long illness. Born in Swansea on October 1, 1923, he became the most expensive forward in Britain in 1950, when the 'Bank of England' club Sunderland paid Aston Villa £30,000 for him. He was one of the game's earliest 'whistle blowers', exposing in his book *I Lead the Attack* (1957) an 'under the counter' payments scandal. For his trouble he received a Football League ban, but went abroad and had three good years in Holland with PSV Eindhoven. He was a prolific scorer, with 23 goals in 38 games for Wales, and 181 in 348 Football League matches (1946–60).

Despite his football credentials, Ford mischievously stated that his greatest claim to fame took place on the cricket pitch at St Helen's, Swansea, in August 1968. Having taken the field as a substitute fielder for Glamorgan he watched the Nottinghamshire captain Garry Sobers bludgeon a world-record 'six sixes in one over' off the hapless left-arm bowler Malcolm Nash.

FOULKE, WILLIAM HENRY. 'Fatty' Foulke, the gargantuan goalkeeper who delighted Victorian and Edwardian football crowds, died of cirrhosis on May 1, 1916, aged 42, in Sister Tate's nursing home in Sheffield. Born in Dawley, Shropshire, on April 12, 1874, he moved to Blackwell in his adopted Derbyshire when a small child. In summer 1900 he played cricket for Derbyshire, but earned his celebrity keeping goal (1894–1907). Sheffield United, Chelsea and Bradford City all benefited from his services and he won one cap for England in 1897.

His range of nicknames – 'Fatty', the 'Blackwell Giant', the 'Leviathan', and the facetious 'Little Willie' – belied the fact that he had once been 'tall and lean'. He first lost his figure at Sheffield United, and at Chelsea topped the scales at almost 24 stone. The newly formed Stamford Bridge outfit emphasised his bulk through shameless publicity stunts, positioning tiny urchins (the first ever ballboys) behind his goal for comedic effect. Now and again Foulke would bring the house down by tucking one under each arm.

For his size he was remarkably nimble. *Association Football and the Men Who Made It* recorded in 1906: 'A football wonder is Willie, the most talked-of player in the world, a leviathan with the agility of a bantam, always the cheeriest of companions, and as difficult to score against in repartee as when between the posts.'

Stories of his antics are legion – breaking the crossbar, rampaging naked in search of the referee after a Cup Final, eating eleven breakfasts at one sitting – but the ubiquitous tale that 'he ended his days pathetically, facing penalties in a "Beat the Goalie" booth on Blackpool front' is without foundation. His biography *Colossus* (2005) says 'he did it for fun on a single afternoon' and that in fact he ran a thriving corner shop in Sheffield, and for some time kept a pub.

In 355 games he conceded 463 goals and won more than he lost. His grave in Sheffield's Burngreave Cemetery – shared with his wife Beatrice – displays a suitably droll motto: 'We cannot Lord thy purpose see, but all is well that's done by thee!'

FRANKLAND, ALFRED, a former draughtsman at the Dick, Kerr engineering company in Preston, died aged 75 on October 9, 1957. He would later be christened 'The Father of Women's Football' in recognition of his 40-year service to the legendary Dick, Kerr Ladies side – also known as Preston Ladies – whose games for charity from the 1920s onwards attracted large crowds.

Born in 1882, Alf Frankland became manager and organiser of the Ladies' works side soon after they were formed in 1917. During his tenure the team played 748 matches, won 702, drew 33 and lost only 13, raising £150,000 for charity whilst under Frankland's personal stewardship.

Known as 'Pop' Frankland, he imposed upon his lady charges the strictest standards of behaviour, but his own personal conduct was later impugned. The club history *In a League of Their Own* (1994) suggests his interpretation of 'personal expenses' was as liberal as it proved lucrative. No damning evidence survives, however, for after Frankland's death his son Ronald hastily destroyed the club accounts which his father had closely guarded for so many years.

Dick, Kerr Ladies played on for a further eight seasons after he died, fulfilling their 828th and final fixture on August 21, 1965, when the Midlands side Hardy Angles met with a 4–0 defeat.

G

GALLACHER, HUGH KILPATRICK, an all-time-great centre-forward, committed suicide at Low Fell, Gateshead, on June 11, 1957, the day before he was due to appear in court on charges of maltreating his son. Born in Bellshill, North Lanarkshire, on February 2, 1903, he rose to prominence with Airdrie. On moving to Newcastle United (1925) he captained them to the 1926–27 League Championship. At Chelsea (1930–34) his appetite for drink, gambling and women cemented his reputation as football's first celebrity 'bad boy', and at Derby County (1934–35) he was allocated a 'minder' to keep him out of trouble.

Capped 20 times for Scotland, he scored a remarkable 24 goals for his country, and was one of the famous 'Wembley Wizards' who inflicted a 5–1 home defeat on England in 1928. Described as 'a pocket-sized forward, whose muscular strength and natural skill make him a brilliant marksman', he is the only Scotland player to have scored five goals in a single international. He wound down his career with a series of short engagements, and retired in 1939 with a remarkable record of 463 goals in 624 first-class games.

No footballer took his own life more emphatically. At 12.08 p.m. on a bright June day he stepped in front of the Edinburgh–York express train and his decapitated body was found 100 yards down the line at Dead Man's Crossing. The tragic end of the 'King of Tyneside' was reported in the *Newcastle Journal* under a stark headline – 'Hughie of the magic feet is dead'.

GEORGE V, H.M. KING, died at Sandringham House, Norfolk, on January 20, 1936. His attendance at an England v. Scotland international in 1909, when Prince of Wales, marked the first appearance at a major game by royalty, and in 1914 he became the first reigning monarch to attend the FA Cup Final: Burnley's 1–0 win over Liverpool, the last played at the Crystal Palace. When opening the Empire Stadium in 1923 – at its famously over-crowded first FA Cup Final – his appearance just before kick-off was held to be a key factor in preventing a major tragedy, a distinction His Majesty shares with Billy the Horse (q.v.). His presentation of the Cup to the Bolton Wanderers captain from the royal box inaugurated a celebrated Wembley tradition. It was also from Wembley that he made the first live radio broadcast by a British sovereign, when he opened the 1924 Empire Exhibition.

His interest in football was a cosmetic one, his patronage of the game being labelled 'a gentle embracing of popular entertainment in an increasingly democratic age'. His own 'sport' was shooting – on December 18, 1913 he killed over 1,000 pheasants in six hours – and his favoured leisure pursuit stamp collecting. His Majesty was born at Marlborough House on June 3, 1865, and was in his 71st year at the time of his death.

GILLIAT, THE REV. WALTER EVELYN, an Anglican minister born in Stoke Poges, Buckinghamshire, on July 22, 1869, died aged 93 on January 2, 1963. An inside-right for Charterhouse School, Oxford University, Old Carthusians and Woking, he is one of over 300 men to have played only once for England (in the 6–1 defeat of Ireland in 1893). He is distinguished from the also-rans, however, not only by his religious calling, but for scoring a hat-trick in his solitary outing, a feat achieved in 20 first-half minutes. He was said to be 'slight of frame, but could vie with the best when fully fit'. He played cricket for Buckinghamshire, and was grandfather to the Hampshire captain Richard Gilliat (1971–78), who also skippered Oxford University at both cricket and soccer.

GIRAUDOUX, HIPPOLYTE 'JEAN', the French novelist, essayist and playwright, born in the village of Bellac on October 29, 1882, died in Paris on January 31, 1944, aged 61. Jean Giraudoux's perceptive observations on life extended to the activity he christened 'the King of sports and the King of games'. In his essay *La Gloire du Football* (1933) he advanced the earliest incisive rationale for the game's worldwide success, and in particular its eclipse of rugby – namely that it is played with a round ball which is conveyed by the feet.

He wrote: 'The ball is that thing which most easily escapes from the laws of life. It has the quality of some capricious force not yet fully tamed. Football owes its global popularity to the fact that it endows the ball with its full potential, for the team imparts to it the activation of 11 shrewd minds and 11 imaginations, with sublime results.' He articulated what generations of 'bag of wind' detractors have failed to grasp, that to give such beauteous life to the ball solely through the art of footwork is a magical thing indeed: 'If the hands have been barred from the game, it is because their intrusion would make the ball no longer a ball, the player no longer a player. The hands are cheats, given only to man and monkey, and the ball does not permit cheating, but only the miraculous effects achieved by sleight of foot alone.' He is buried in Passy Cemetery, Paris.

GOODHART, HARRY CHESTER, three times England centre-forward (1883), died aged 36 on April 21, 1895, after a bout of influenza. Born in Wimbledon on July 17, 1858, he won two FA Cup medals with Old Etonians (1879 and 1882) and scored five hat-tricks in the competition. He lectured in classics at Trinity College, Cambridge (1884–90), and was appointed in 1891 to the Latin Chair at Edinburgh. Uniquely for an England striker he is associated with the debate concerning the identity of 'Jack the Ripper', for Goodhart was a close friend and confidante of no fewer than two nominated suspects.

The lesser-known – the poet James Kenneth Stephen – he was at Eton with. Stephen's stanza 'We played together in football weather, and messed together for years' celebrated their comradeship, which continued at Cambridge.

The more notorious was Edward Prince of Wales, afterwards Duke of Clarence, whom Goodhart tutored at Cambridge. The two became such intimates that in 1886 the Prince was best man at Goodhart's wedding. Since James Stephen had also tutored Prince Edward previously, the close-knit trio have been well scrutinised by Ripper enthusiasts, although no sinister act has ever been attributed to Goodhart. When the former England front man was buried at Lower Beeding Church, Horsham, Sussex, a friend said: 'He combined the artist's brain with the skill and strength of an artisan.'

GOODYEAR, CHARLES, the American inventor born in New Haven, Connecticut, on December 29, 1800, died in New York on July 1, 1860, never to know that his passion for rubber technology would enable the rudimentary pastime of football to evolve into 'the world's greatest game'.

At the time of his demise inflated pig bladders had for centuries served as a football's innards, but their inherent weakness and irregular shape precluded the mass manufacture of a robust sphere capable of uniform bounce. Although synthetic rubber bladders had been experimented with, these were found to perish in cold weather and were not waterproof – hence football had remained hidebound by technological stagnancy, the development of skilled ball manipulation being stifled as a consequence.

In 1839 Goodyear discovered the vulcanisation process by which rubber could be made to retain stability and elasticity. He patented his findings in June 1844, and in 1852 introduced his ideas to the Manchester-based company founded by Glasgow-born Charles Macintosh. Although best known for its near-eponymous 'Mackintosh' raincoat the firm soon became the world's first mass producer of rubber football bladders. When cased in leather – hence the archaic term a 'case-ball' or the vernacular 'casey' – the result was what one chronicler described as 'the perfect sphere for the perfect game'. In such a fashion the primitive act of kicking was speedily elevated to what the Victorians dubbed 'the art of pedipulation' – and in 1863, three years after Goodyear died, the Football Association was formed.

Yet the inventor was deep in debt at his death, since unscrupulous rivals had exploited the vagaries of the patent system for their own ends. His poignant demise occurred while travelling to visit his dying daughter in New York. On his arrival she had already passed away, and Goodyear collapsed and died shortly afterwards at the Fifth Avenue Hotel, aged 59.

Some consider it ironic that association football should owe so much to an American, yet it is decidedly the case that the global game could not have taken the great strides it did but for the discovery of vulcanisation. A colleague bestowed upon Charles Goodyear a laudatory epitaph: 'He devoted his life to bringing the benefits of rubber to humankind.' The patent number that changed the world was 3,633.

GRACIE, CPL. THOMAS, a prolific marksman for Heart of Midlothian, born in Yorkhill, Glasgow, on June 12, 1889, and Europe's leading scorer in 1914–15, died aged 26 of leukaemia on October 23, 1915, in Stobhill Hospital, Glasgow.

The son of a master butcher, he qualified as a bookkeeper and worked as a meat salesman while pursuing his football career. After joining Airdrie (1907) he moved swiftly to Hamilton and then Morton (1909), but following a bizarre incident involving the club mascot Toby the lamb (q.v.) he was sold to Everton in 1911. He played only 13 games before changing allegiance to Liverpool, but soon expressed himself 'unappreciated' in England – his clever play was thought 'too scientific' – and moved to Heart of Midlothian for £400 in May 1914.

Unrest in Europe rendered the move inopportune – along with other Hearts players Gracie joined the 'Heart of Midlothian Battalion', a volunteer force dubbed 'the McCrae's' which was raised in Edinburgh soon after the war began.

In March 1915, shortly before his military training began in earnest, Gracie was diagnosed with a serious illness but told no one except his manager. He continued to play football 'for the good of the side' and remarkably finished the Scottish League's highest scorer for 1914–15 – indeed his 29-goal haul was not bettered anywhere in Europe.

During manoeuvres in Ripon, Yorkshire, after the season closed, his condition worsened and he was transported back to his family home in Glasgow. *McCrae's Battalion* (2003) quotes the Hearts shareholder Sir James Leishman, who visited Gracie in his last few days: 'He admitted to me he played and trained when he should have been confined to bed. He had that quiet resolution and courage which makes men like him hang on until they drop. I feel convinced that he would have proved a first-class fighting man.'

On October 26, 1915, Tommy Gracie was laid to rest at Glasgow's Craigton Cemetery, within sight of Rangers' Ibrox Park, where only the year before he had starred in a famous victory.

GREEN, GEOFFREY, who died on May 9, 1990, aged 78, was an eminent football writer known as 'the godfather of football reporting'. He began writing for *The Times* in the 1930s, serving as its football correspondent for 40 years. While articulating events with both eloquence and fervour he seldom lost touch with the common fan.

His report of England's shock 6–3 defeat by Hungary at Wembley in 1953 described 'the inventors of the game' as 'strangers in a strange world'. Of the England captain Billy Wright's comic attempts to contain Puskas, he wrote that he 'flew into the tackle like a fire engine going in the wrong direction for the blaze'. He wrote scholarly official histories of both the FA Cup (1949) and the Football Association (1953) and also penned a tribute to his favourite Manchester club – *There's Only One United* (1978).

Green won his soccer blue at Cambridge University after attending Shrewsbury School, where his taste for academia was conspicuously eclipsed by his love of sport. On revisiting his *alma mater* in the 1960s, his former classics master Jimmy Street greeted him: 'My dear Green, every morning I read you in the paper, and every morning I'm astonished how you do it. At school you were such a perfect combination of doltish imperfections that you could hardly write your name at the top of an examination paper.' Green's muttered riposte, 'Pardon me for living', was later chosen by him as the title for his autobiography.

GREENWOOD, DOCTOR HAYDOCK, was born in Blackburn on October 31, 1860, and died in Buxton, Derbyshire, on November 3, 1951, aged 91. He played for Malvern College (1878–79), Blackburn Rovers and Corinthians, and in 1882 was capped twice by England. Described as 'a strong-kicking full-back who is sometimes slow', his curious name Doctor stood for no medical or other learned qualification – he was christened thus, and in later life became an agriculturalist.

GRIBBLE, LEONARD REGINALD, the British criminologist and fiction writer, born on February 1, 1908 in London, died on September 27, 1985, aged 77. His legacy to football was two stirring novels – *The Arsenal Stadium Mystery* (1939) and *They Kidnapped Stanley Matthews* (1950) – both vehicles for Gribble's series character Superintendent Anthony Slade. The former book was quickly adapted into what later became a cult film.

His family hailed from Barnstaple, Devon, and in 1932 he married Nancy Mason. During the war he served in the Press and Censorship Division of the Ministry of Information in London and he was a founding member of the Crime Writers' Association (1953). Critics have labelled his books lightweight, overly sensational or even lurid, but Gribble maintained his sole aim was to entertain.

Among his classics are *The Stolen Home Secretary* (1932), *King Spiv* (1948), *The Frightened Chameleon* (1950) and *Sex Marks the Spot* (1954). His most celebrated contribution to serious criminology was a 1973 article in *True Detective* titled 'Was Jack the Ripper a Black Magician'?

Leonard Gribble wrote well over 100 books in a variety of guises – his pen names included Sterry Browning, James Gannett, Leo Grex, Piers Marlowe, Dexter Muir, Louis Grey and Bruce Sanders. He ended his career with *The Dead Don't Scream* (1983) and passed away almost unnoticed two years later.

GUNN, WILLIAM, who was born on December 4, 1858, one of few Englishmen to win full international honours at both football and cricket, died of cancer aged 62 on January 29, 1921, in his native Nottingham. His 6ft 3in frame was said to be 'a sight to behold', the more conspicuous since Gunn often played as a winger, his loping run being likened by one observer to that of 'a stag breaking cover'. He played a solitary game for Nottingham Forest before changing allegiance to Notts County (1881–92) and twice representing England (1884). Gunn's party piece was a prodigious one-armed throw-in which enabled him to launch the ball into the danger zone from almost any part of the touchline – this rare skill precipitated the introduction of compulsory two-handed throws from 1882.

His celebrated cricket career embraced Nottinghamshire (1880–1904) and 11 Test matches (1887–99). His nephews

George and John also played cricket for Nottinghamshire and England.

In later life Billy Gunn was a Notts County director, and at the time of his death was vice-president of the club. The sports correspondent James Catton wrote: 'Utterly sound and impregnable where honour was concerned, he was a man of great deeds and not a jot of littleness or a tittle of crankiness.' He left the large sum of £57,932, amassed through the famous sports equipment firm Gunn & Moore, which he co-founded in 1885.

GWYNNE, THE RT. REV. BISHOP LLEWELLYN HENRY. When he died aged 94 in Epsom, Surrey, on December 3, 1957, an assembly of 1,300 attended his Westminster Abbey memorial service. Born in Kilvey, near Swansea, on June 11, 1863, he was Derby County's centre-forward between 1887 and 1888, and captain once. Some years earlier when a young curate he nurtured the future England star Steve Bloomer (q.v.), a member of his choirboy team.

After parish work in Nottingham he went to Khartoum as a missionary. Later, when Bishop of Sudan and Egypt (1920–46), his frequent use of air travel around his see earned him the sobriquet 'The Flying Bishop'. Many areas of North Africa benefited from his guidance, his death marking the passing of an era in the history of the British in Sudan. Perhaps his proudest boast was scoring four goals on Christmas Eve – the only bishop ever to do so for a first-class club – when he bagged a double brace for Derby County against Eckington in 1887.

HAMMOND, WALTER REGINALD, the celebrated Gloucestershire and
England cricketer, died of a heart attack aged 62 on July 1, 1965, in
Kloof, Natal, South Africa, where he had emigrated. 'Wally'
Hammond is one of only three men – along with Brian Close and
Ian Botham – to skipper England in a Test match and play professional football. A forward with Bristol Rovers (1921–23), he
scored two goals in 20 League games. One of the greatest of all
cricketers, his first-class batting average (1920–51) exceeded 50 in
both Test and county games.

Labelled 'shy and aloof' by colleagues, he suffered endless
cruel innuendo after contracting a 'mystery illness' in the West
Indies in the 1920s. Although he reputedly had a form of
syphilis, Hammond always maintained that he had sustained 'a
mosquito bite in the groin area'. Born in Dover, Kent, on June 19,
1903, he spent part of his childhood in China before attending
Cirencester Grammar School. He died poorly off, a benefit fund
being raised in Gloucestershire to aid his widow. His superior
brand of sporting prowess earned him the dubious sobriquet
'Majesty'.

HANCOCKS, JOHN, the 5ft 4in right-winger, born in Oakengates,
Shropshire, on April 30, 1919, died on February 19, 1994. The
'small man with a big heart' won three England caps and lasting
adulation at Wolverhampton Wanderers (1946–56) – his 168
goals in 378 games a prodigious return for a wingman. It is said no
England player had smaller feet. Attendant supporter scepticism
was routinely circumvented via a positive spin to his pen-picture:
'Johnny Hancocks has a never-say-die spirit, his size two in

footwear presenting no bar to the rapid movement and blistering shooting which have become his trademark.'

HARDEN, LEO, was born in Hartlepool on May 7, 1923, and his death there aged 76 on December 5, 1999, prompted the rarefied headline 'A Hartlepool United Legend'. In 180 matches for his only first-class club he hit 52 goals, scoring on both his 1946 debut and in his farewell game ten years later.

One of the Third Division North's great characters, he remained a part-time player throughout his professional career and earned his living by driving a dustcart. He took the attendant jibes in good part – to terrace wags yelling 'rubbish Harden' he would retort by threatening to leave their bins full. His chief weapons were lightning speed and a rasping shot – the *Hartlepool Mail* said of one of his goals that 'only the net prevented the ball from demolishing the Queen's Road dance hall as well'.

His most celebrated game was the 6–0 home win over Rochdale in October 1953. Selected as a late replacement Harden was plucked from the pub shortly before kick-off. Still smelling of Best Bitter he scored four and made the other two. He had one of the best nicknames in football – 'The Flying Dustman'.

HARDING, MATTHEW, the 42-year-old vice-chairman of Chelsea FC, died on October 22, 1996, when his helicopter plunged into a field near Middlewich, Cheshire. He had been returning from his side's Coca Cola Cup tie at Bolton Wanderers. Born in Haywards Heath, Sussex, on December 26, 1953, he attended Abingdon School, Oxfordshire, where he shunned the ruling rugby ethos in favour of football. In 1994 he ploughed £26.5 million of his insurance business fortune into his beloved Chelsea. The move led to a bitter feud with the club chairman Ken Bates.

Although born into privilege – the son of a Lloyd's under-writer – Harding became an avowed socialist. A devotee of Bob

Dylan, he was given to quoting the cynical pronouncements of Holden Caulfield – the 'angry young man' in J.D. Salinger's *Catcher in the Rye* – who looked down upon the elite world he occupied while himself overtly displaying some of the very characteristics he so despised. Harding preferred to mix with 'real fans' rather than corporate types. His favourite pre-match refreshment was Guinness and oysters.

He was survived by his estranged wife Ruth, their three sons and one daughter, and a daughter by his girlfriend Vicky Jaramillo. His death prompted disparate reaction. The balloonist Per Lindstrand said: 'He was a "mission impossible" type. The word "cannot" wasn't in his vocabulary – he was totally unafraid and carefree.' Ken Bates said: 'He was an evil man.' The North Stand at Stamford Bridge was renamed the Matthew Harding Stand in his memory.

HAWKES, ROBERT MURRAY, the first Luton Town player capped by his country, died aged 64 on September 12, 1945. Born in Breachwood Green, near Luton, on October 18, 1880, he served the Hatters from 1901 until 1920, much of the time as captain. Ranked amongst the finest left-halves of the era, he won five full England caps (1907–08) and 22 amateur caps, gaining a gold medal with the Great Britain XI at the 1908 London Olympics. His achievements might merit no particular attention but for the curious observation made in a pen-picture that 'he wore a metal plate under his auburn hair, which accounted for an apparent disinclination to head the ball'. Considered a Luton Town all-time great, he was by vocation a straw-hat maker.

HAWTREY, JOHN PURVIS, born at Eton on July 19, 1850, died on August 17, 1925, in Hammersmith, London. Educated at Eton and then Clifton College (a rugby establishment) he did not altogether take to 'soccer' at first, but his latent prowess as a custodian surfaced with Remnants, who in 1877 partook of three rounds of the English Cup before their colours were finally lowered. In 1879, when with Old Etonians, Hawtrey gained his sole Cup winner's medal, keeping his goal intact in a 1–0 defeat of Clapham Rovers.

The Sportsman summed up his goalkeeping ability pithily – 'he is a good one' and 'very fine' – but others noted 'his inconsistency of form'. He played twice for England and was besides a useful cricketer and member of M.C.C. He was first a schoolmaster in Slough, then in turn actor, producer and playwright – this last under the *nom de plume* John Trent-Hay – but finally went into journalism and became editor of the *Sporting World* newspaper.

His brother was the celebrated Victorian stage actor – a mentor to Noel Coward – Sir Charles Hawtrey. In a later era the aspiring thespian George Frederick Joffre Hartree, who had read the star's memoirs, decided to take up 'Charles Hawtrey' as a stage name, thereby establishing a curious link between the 1879 Cup Final and the *Carry On* films in which he starred. Through roles such as Private Widdle and the camp lavatory designer Charles Coote the latter-day Hawtrey became a cult figure in cinema, while his footballer 'phantom brother' John Purvis Hawtrey is all but forgotten.

HEGINBOTHAM, STAFFORD, the toy manufacturer and larger-than-life former chairman of Bradford City AFC, died on April 21, 1995, aged 61. Born on September 12, 1933, he took the chair in October 1965 at the unusually young age of 32, imposing an ebullient personality on every facet of the club.

When Bradford faced the prospect of oblivion in 1983 he funded a revival which saw them become Third Division champions in 1984–85. In expansive mood he delivered a famous quote – 'Football is the opera of the people' – only to endure a terrible tragedy soon afterwards. On May 11, 1985, during the 'promotion celebration' game against Lincoln City, the ancient Main Stand at Valley Parade was destroyed by a fire in which 56 perished. His words on this occasion were tearfully sombre – 'This was to be our day'.

He stepped down on health grounds three years later and had already died when City won promotion to the Premiership in 1998–99. He is immortalised in the cheery persona of the rotund mascot 'City Gent' for which Heginbotham was the original inspiration.

HENRY VIII, H.M. KING, died aged 55 at the Palace of Whitehall on January 28, 1547, in the 38th year of his turbulent reign. Although mainly associated with a voracious appetite, corpulent figure and a multitude of wives, Henry occupies an unexpected and primary position in the timeline of football history.

An inventory records that in 1526, when aged 35, the monarch commanded his Great Wardrobe to supply boots made especially for football, this being the earliest-known specific reference to such attire. The ankle-high, hand-made leather football boots cost four shillings (today's equivalent of £100) and were stitched together by Cornelius Johnson, official cordwainer to His Majesty.

Henry was born at Greenwich on June 28, 1491. Although obese in later years – he had a 54-inch waist – he was in his youth a lithe and athletic character, 6ft 2in tall, who engaged in sporting pursuits with no little vigour. A favourite was jousting, by which means in 1536 he suffered a serious thigh injury, his further exercise being thus curtailed with attendant consequences.

Only two of his six wives outlived him – Catherine Parr and Anne of Cleves – but another is linked to the *curiosa* of football. The Boleyn Ground – the official title of West Ham United's home Upton Park – takes its name from a turreted sixteenth-century house known as Boleyn Castle, which once stood adjacent to the site and was named for its links to Henry's beheaded second wife Anne Boleyn. Henry's football boots are known to have survived him, but are now lost.

HERON, CHARLES FRANCIS WILLIAM, a wine merchant and England forward – described as 'an excellent dribbler but rather too light' – died on October 23, 1914, in Southall, Middlesex, aged 61. Born at Uxbridge Common on September 10, 1853, Frank Heron's sole international cap was against Scotland on March 4, 1876, when his brother Hubert also played. Two weeks later they both collected FA Cup winner's medals with Wanderers. No England player has left a more peculiar will. Heron said: 'Though not wishing to be kept unnecessarily long after my decease, I should like my dear ones to be absolutely certain that I am dead before I am screwed down. The reason for this desire is obvious.'

HERRIOT, JAMES, OBE, the veterinary surgeon, author of the popular *All Creatures Great and Small* stories, died on February 23, 1995, at his home in Thirlby, Yorkshire, the county in which he had ministered to animals for half a century. His name was a pseudonym – he was born James Alfred Wight on October 3, 1916, in Sunderland, but was brought up in Glasgow where he qualified as a veterinary surgeon in 1939.

After his oeuvre began with *If Only They Could Talk* (1970) his ensuing celebrity as an author must be partially apportioned to his passion for football. Forbidden by the rules of the veterinary profession to write commercially under his own name, he chose that belonging to the Scotland international goalkeeper Jim Herriot, after seeing him play for Birmingham City in a televised game against Manchester United.

James Herriot's books sold 50 million copies in 20 countries. His decision to retire as a vet was made whilst stitching up a cut in a cow's teat. Jim Herriot played eight times for Scotland (1968–69) and decided to retire as a goalkeeper after joining Morton in 1976–77. The author died aged 78 after suffering from prostate cancer – the footballer survived him and remains by proxy the only Scotland goalkeeper successfully to perform a hysterectomy on a cat.

HIGHAM, GEORGE GARNET, a pioneer of football in Wales, lost his life in spectacular fashion at Drwysynant, near Dolgellau, Merionethshire, on October 20, 1925. Although twice playing full-back for Wales in the late 1870s, his chief celebrity was as co-founder in 1875 of the Oswestry Football Club, with which he remained associated as player and committee member for almost 50 years. He was born in the Shropshire town in 1855 and kept a sports outfitter's shop there, although by profession a gunsmith.

On the day of his death he had been out for a drive in his Austin Seven with his second wife Sarah when the car was found overturned in a river. The couple had drowned but police were unable to discover how the tragic accident occurred. Higham was then aged 70 and perhaps his faculties had diminished – in his prime he was praised for his 'fine footwork and impeccable judgment'.

HOBY, LADY ELIZABETH, a woman of great learning, died in May 1609, aged 81, at her Berkshire seat Bisham Abbey, which centuries later was used by the England football team for its get-togethers. Thought to have been born at Gidea Hall, Romford, in 1528, she is therefore the first Essex girl sensationally linked to the England camp, for on a number of occasions her materialised form has made unbidden nocturnal visits to the squad.

Through selfishness she brought about the death of her young son, and lived out her life in remorse, which continued after she died. The ancient manor house is reputed to be haunted by her tortured spirit, which has been seen, heard and felt by visitors. While on a visit to Bisham with Derby County the highly strung England goalkeeper Reg Matthews refused to enter the building on account of his rabid fear of ghosts.

Her Ladyship is most often only heard – emitting a dolorous moan from a distant room – but sometimes appears in negative form, with black face and white clothes, in the act of washing her hands. Witnesses have stated that: 'She tears curtains from windows, throws things around, and causes untold mayhem in the small hours.'

A number of destructive acts which have occurred at Bisham Abbey in the presence of the England squad have been solemnly ascribed by the players to the unfortunate Elizabeth Hoby. She outlived two husbands and was buried in Bisham Church on June 2, 1609, where a lavish monument to her memory may still be seen.

HOCKEY, TREVOR, a football nomad, one of the game's most colourful characters and the first 'Anglo' to play legitimately for Wales – gaining nine caps between 1972 and 1974 – died aged 43 on April 2, 1987, in Keighley, Yorkshire. Born there on May 1, 1943, he signed professional for Bradford City in 1960. Although initially a winger he made his lasting mark as a ball-winning midfielder, whose combative style often brought him into conflict with referees – in Poland in 1973 he became the first Welshman dismissed while playing for his country.

At his principal club Birmingham City (195 League appearances 1965–71) he became one of few players bold enough to release a solo record, 'Happy 'Cos I'm Blue', but soon afterwards adopted the red and white stripes of Second Division Sheffield United, where he played a crucial role in their late promotion push in 1971–72.

He was by then a cult figure whose full beard and long hair earned him the nickname 'Dai Fungus'. Those offended by his tackling dubbed him 'the wild man' or 'werewolf' and it was rare for him to complete a game without being subjected at least once to the quaint admonishment 'Hockey you hairy get'.

He qualified to play for Wales because his father – a former rugby league player with Keighley – was born at Abertillery. His career record was 521 League games and 28 goals for seven clubs over 16 seasons. Tragically, the enthusiasm which characterised his approach to life may have precipitated his death – he died of a heart attack while still in his kit shortly after taking part in a five-a-side tournament in Keighley. He was thought to be the only professional footballer to own a pink piano.

HOGG, QUINTIN, the English merchant, philanthropist and founder of the Polytechnic movement, died on January 17, 1903, in London, where he had been born on February 14, 1845. Known at Eton as 'Piggy Hogg' he was in common with many Etonians a pioneer of association football. Both a goalkeeper and full-back, he made 31 appearances for Wanderers FC (winners of the first FA Cup) between 1865 and 1870, and through ancestry twice represented Scotland in the pseudo-internationals of 1870 and 1871 against England.

   He made a fortune trading tea and sugar but salved his conscience by opening 'ragged schools' for the poor children of London, to whom with his wife Alice he devoted much attention. In 1882 he founded Regent Street Polytechnic and died there in his own apartment aged 57 – he was found slumped lifeless in his bath, the tragedy being attributed to a poorly ventilated gas stove. His memorial in Portland Place was for many years the only statue in London to incorporate a football. His grandson Quintin Hogg (1907–2001) – the Tory politician Lord Hailsham – was Lord Chancellor in Mrs Thatcher's administration.

HOOMAN, THOMAS CHARLES, the Portland cement manufacturer and former merchant ship broker, lost his battle for life at 6 Marine Parade, Hythe, Kent, on September 22, 1938, following an operation. The 87-year-old began his life at The Copse, Hoo Lane, Kidderminster, Worcestershire, on December 28, 1850, and had been a fine all-round sportsman.

   When in the Wanderers side which won the first FA Cup Final

in 1872 he was described as 'a fine forward, kicks well and is the fastest dribbler of the day'. In four pre-official international matches he represented England against Scotland, but when the call twice came in 1872–73 for him to win his full colours he declared himself 'unavailable' on each occasion. One of the first men to decline an invitation to play for his country, he was never selected again.

At cricket he headed the batting averages for Charterhouse School in 1867–68. He ran in the sprint for England in 1872 and rowed in the Grand Final at Henley for Kingston. He was besides a good boxer, marksman and golfer, and father of the Walker Cup golfer and Kent cricketer C.V.L. Hooman.

His *Times* obituary revealed something of the forward's instinct in his nature, stating that shortly before his death he conducted an interview in which he claimed to have scored the winning goal in the 1872 Cup Final. It appears he had little anticipated that assiduous statisticians would later place that honour securely at the feet of Morton Peto Betts (q.v.) – or perhaps, in his dotage, the old forward's memory had merely dimmed.

HORSE, BILLY (THE), football's most esteemed equine figure, also known as 'Billie', departed this life on December 15, 1930, aged 20. On April 28, 1923, under the charge of PC George Scorey of Rochester Row police station, Billy was instrumental in clearing encroaching crowds from the Empire Stadium turf, so enabling the first Wembley FA Cup Final to kick off only 45 minutes late after postponement had appeared inevitable. Bolton Wanderers beat West Ham United 2–0.

Although one of several horses on duty, black and white news images of the near calamity emphasised Billy's stark colouring. The occasion was duly dubbed 'The White Horse Final', although in a newspaper interview some years later Constable Scorey was at pains to point out that 'Billy was actually a grey.'

In 2006 BBC Radio Five Live listeners polled that a footbridge at the new Wembley Stadium should be named 'White Horse Bridge' – Sir Alf Ramsey came second – a tribute which added to one already made following Billy's sad passing. On that occasion Sir Percy Laurie, head of the Metropolitan Mounted Branch, presented Constable Scorey with a polished and mounted hoof from his dead former steed.

HOUSEMAN, PETER, the Chelsea star, is perhaps the only footballer to have both a youth league and a recreation ground named after him, the honours being bestowed following his untimely death in a car crash near Oxford on March 20, 1977, when only 31. A classy left-winger in Chelsea's 'Golden Years' of the late 1960s and early 1970s, he was hugely influential as both scorer and provider in the club's celebrated 1970 FA Cup-winning campaign. Among a glamour-packed group of players dubbed 'Kings of the King's Road' he was the quiet man, said to be 'modest to a fault, a model pro, and a real player's player', although on occasions cruelly barracked for his apparent distaste for a healthy challenge.

Born in Battersea on Christmas Eve 1945, he played 343 competitive matches for Chelsea (1963–75), scoring 39 goals and laying on countless more for Peter Osgood and Ian Hutchinson. He had made 72 appearances for Oxford United (1975–77) before being killed with his wife Sally when driving home from a fundraising event, their three sons all under eight being thus orphaned. He was nicknamed 'Nobby' by his Chelsea colleagues, two of whom also died far too soon – Hutchinson (54) and Osgood (59).

HOWELL, LEONARD SIDGWICK, who died in Lausanne, Switzerland, on September 7, 1895, was educated at Winchester College and filled the left full-back berth in the historic first official victory of the England football side, a 4–2 triumph over Scotland at the Kennington Oval on March 8, 1873. It was only the second full international match played anywhere in the world, and the first in England, but proved to be Howell's solitary cap.

Only three weeks later he won an FA Cup winner's medal with Wanderers, *The Football Annual* praising his 'unwearied defence and unvarying precision', noting that 'his kicking not infrequently brings the house down'. Injury presently ended his soccer days, but he became an accomplished cricketer – with 519 runs for Surrey (1869–80) at an average of 18.53 – and a member of M.C.C.

L.S. Howell was a malt factor by profession. Although a fine sportsman he was not enduringly robust – born at Herne Hill, London, on August 6, 1848, he had attained only 47 years when death mockingly assailed him at a Swiss health resort.

HOWELL, RABY, the England international born on October 12, 1867, in the hamlet of Wincobank, between Sheffield and Rotherham, died aged 69 in 1937. The son of a horse-dealer who sold pots and pans, he was born in a Romany caravan and is the only full-blooded gypsy to play for England.

Known in the game as 'Rabbi' he first pursued the leather in earnest for the Sheffield club Ecclesfield, and also assisted Rotherham Swifts before joining Sheffield United in 1890 for ten shillings a week. At first a centre-forward, then a half-back, he stood only 5ft 5in but was said to be 'hard as nails'. His Sheffield United colleague Ernest 'Nudger' Needham recalled: 'A gypsy by birth, "Rab" perhaps owes some of his inexhaustible vitality to his lucky parentage. No man is more untiring. He rejoices at meeting the best of forward wings, and should the outside man indulge in dribbling he sticks to him like a leech.'

He played twice for England – four years apart in 1895 and 1899 – and was with Sheffield United when they gained their first League Championship in 1897–98. After 240 appearances and 11 goals he departed the club in unsavoury circumstances. After he scored two own goals in an away game at Sunderland, the Sheffield committee suspected Howell may have been bribed and let him go to Liverpool for £200. He later joined Preston North End, where in 1903 his eventful career was ended by a broken leg.

HUDSON, JOSEPH, was born in Birmingham in 1848 and died there in 1930 aged 82. Through innovatory thinking the labourer's son secured a spiritual presence in world football which yet remains. In 1884 in a small workshop at his end-of-terrace home in St Mark's Square, Birmingham, he invented the world's first reliable pea whistle, later named the 'Acme Thunderer'.

It quickly replaced the frantically waved handkerchief as the favoured tool for match control, and the iconic brand has been vociferously employed by referees ever since. By the year 2000 J. Hudson and Co. Ltd of Birmingham had sold over 200 million 'Acme Thunderer' whistles in 119 countries. Most football matches played anywhere in the world are still controlled by Joseph Hudson's humble invention.

Those not best disposed towards the refereeing fraternity might consider the whistle ill-christened – its name derives from the Greek *akme* meaning 'highest level of attainment'.

HUGH, 'LITTLE SAINT' OF LINCOLN, a nine-year-old English Christian who disappeared on July 31, 1255 – his body being discovered down a well on August 29 of the same year – is according to legend the first boy whose trepidation at asking for his ball back had mortal consequences. The owner of the property where the dead child was found – a Jew named Jopin – confessed under duress that young Hugh had been ritually crucified by prominent Jews who had gone to Lincoln on the pretext of a wedding. He was hanged for the crime.

Jewish leaders considered the charges 'trumped up', but Sir Hugh – as he was then known – was canonised as a Christian martyr and buried with great pomp in Lincoln Cathedral. He lies there still, commemorated by a plaque.

Saint Hugh soon became 'the stuff of legends' and a tale was put about that he had been playing football and was in truth stabbed by the Jew's daughter, who lured the innocent to retrieve his wayward ball. The foul episode was later immortalised in *The Ballad of Hugh of Lincoln*:

> Four and twenty boys
> Were playing at the ba'
> And by it came him sweet sir Hugh,
> And he play'd o'er them a'.
>
> He kick'd the ba' with his right foot,
> And catch'd it wi' his knee,
> And thro the Jew's window
> He saw the bonny ba' flee.
>
> 'Throw down the ba', ye Jew's daughter,
> Throw down the ba' to me!' –
> 'Never a bit', says the Jew's daughter,
> 'Till up to me come ye.'

The ballad extends to 17 verses. Hugh protests – 'I winna come up, I darena come up' – but succumbs to the promise of an apple and is laid on a dressing table and fatally stabbed: 'stickit like a swine'. In 1975 the folk-rock group Steeleye Span recorded a version of 'Little Sir Hugh' on their album *Commoner's Crown*.

In the absence of a patron saint of football Saint Hugh might justly fill the breach. His sorry case is the first instance in which racism and the game were linked, and a salutary example of the alarming consequences of shoddy ball control, especially when showboating.

HULL, RODNEY STEPHEN, the popular light entertainer and celebrity
   Bristol Rovers fan, originally a trained electrician, died aged 63 on
   March 17, 1999, after falling from a ladder whilst trying to adjust
   a television aerial at 'Crutches Farm', his cottage-style bungalow in
   Hastings Road, Winchelsea, near Rye, East Sussex.

   The tragic accident occurred midway through the first half of
   the Champions League fixture at the San Siro Stadium between
   Inter Milan and Manchester United, which twice-married Hull
   had been watching on television. His devastated 19-year-old son
   Oliver, who had been viewing the game with him, was the only
   witness: 'When the picture lost quality my father went up on the
   roof to fix the aerial, something he often did. I was to tell him
   when the signal was good by leaning out of the window and shout-
   ing, but I heard a light thud and then a heavy thud.'

   The 6ft 2in comedy icon had fallen through a period-style
   greenhouse roof onto a concrete floor and was pronounced dead
   on arrival at the Conquest Hospital, Hastings. Despite a patholo-
   gist's report that the star had consumed a quantity of alcohol
   which 'may have slightly impaired his judgement', an inquest later
   pronounced a verdict of accidental death due to a severe skull frac-
   ture and serious chest injuries.

   Rod Hull will be fondly remembered for his arm-length puppet
   'Emu', a mute, highly aggressive bird of the Australian species
   Dromaius Novaehollandiae, which he seldom appeared on stage or
   screen without. The unpredictable bird will be best remembered for
   attacking celebrity Barnsley Football Club fan Michael Parkinson
   during an edition of his eponymous television chat show – also for
   eating the floral bouquet of Her Majesty the Queen Mother when
   introduced at a 1972 Royal Variety Performance.

   In 1993 the British Pipe Smokers' Council named Hull 'Pipe
   Smoker of the Year' and he also bestows a permanent legacy to the
   music industry. After Bristol Rovers won promotion to the Second
   Division in 1973–74 he recorded 'Bristol Rovers All the Way' with

the triumphant squad – a rousing ditty sung to the tune of 'She'll Be Coming Round the Mountain' – which failed to make the charts. Prior to his death he was also the subject of a 'tribute' song by the cult band Half Man Half Biscuit, the 1988 release 'Rod Hull is Alive – Why?'

After his untimely demise genuine tributes came from far and wide. Michael Parkinson described him as 'a very charming and sensitive man – quite unlike the Emu'. Dave Callaghan, a spokesman for the Queen's Head, where Rod was a regular, said: 'He was very intelligent. He could do *The Times* crossword in 20 minutes and did so much for the restoration of Icklesham Church. He never really liked the Emu.' Mr Hull's final game finished Inter Milan 1 Manchester United 1, both goals coming in the second half after he had been taken away by ambulance.

HUME, CARDINAL GEORGE BASIL, OM, the Archbishop of Westminster, spiritual leader of English and Welsh Catholics, and faithful adherent of Newcastle United, died peacefully at the Hospital of St John and St Elizabeth in London, on June 17, 1999, aged 76. He had been suffering from advanced abdominal cancer and had followed the Magpies since 1933–34.

Born George Hume at Newcastle upon Tyne on March 2, 1923, he adopted the name Basil on becoming a monk in the Benedictine Order at Ampleforth, Yorkshire, in 1941. In 1963 he became Abbot of Ampleforth College, holding the office until elevated to Archbishop of Westminster in 1976.

At Oxford University he took part in rugby, football and athletics and at Westminster played what he called 'geriatric squash'. Despite meeting a myriad of world figures – including former amateur goalkeeper Pope John Paul II – his declared 'proudest moment' was getting the autograph of the Newcastle United centre-forward Jackie Milburn when they were created Freemen of the City together in 1980.

Shortly before his death Cardinal Hume was awarded the Order of Merit by the Queen. Of his passing a fellow Newcastle United supporter said: 'He was goodness personified, a true holy man with extraordinary humility and unswerving dedication.' The fan was Prime Minister Tony Blair, whose claim to having 'enjoyed watching Jackie Milburn play at St James's Park' has been said to be, if not exactly 'untrue', certainly 'wanting in chronological veracity'.

The closing line of Cardinal Hume's obituary in the *National Catholic Reporter* read: 'He said he wanted the *Match of the Day* theme music played at his funeral.' The mischievous request went unfulfilled. He was survived by neither a wife nor children, being a lifelong bachelor and staunch upholder of celibacy.

HUNTER, ALEXANDER, secretary from 1883 to 1887 of the Football Association of Wales, died on December 16, 1899, having 12 years earlier contrived to achieve a unique international appearance record. Born the son of a clergyman at Tiverton, Devon, in 1862 – and by profession an architect and surveyor based in Llangollen – Alex Hunter was the only player capped by Wales while also serving as the country's FA secretary.

When the Welsh party travelled to play Ireland in Belfast on March 12, 1887, several players either refused to brave the sea crossing or were rendered unfit by the experience. The 27-year-old Hunter confidently volunteered his services, but this was an unwise move according to a newspaper report: 'Mr Hunter the secretary of the Welsh Association filled the gap in the Welsh team by playing half-back, but it is needless to say it was neither strengthened nor stabilised by his presence. He must have thought it a good joke to get playing international, for whatever his knowledge may be of the theory, he was glaringly deficient in practice.' Ireland gained their first ever international victory – having conceded 96 goals in their 15 previous internationals they humbled Wales by four goals to one.

Alex Hunter later became treasurer of the Welsh FA but severed his administrative links in 1891 and became a referee in the Football Alliance. He moved to Shrewsbury shortly afterwards and when he died there at the young age of 37 was the town's sanitary inspector.

JACK, DAVID BONE NIGHTINGALE, an England captain capped nine times (1924–32), died aged 59 on September 10, 1958, in London. Born in Bolton on April 3, 1899, he was a prolific forward dubbed 'the titan of his age'. His career embraced a notable hat-trick of firsts. With Bolton Wanderers (1920–28) he scored the first ever goal at Wembley Stadium, in their 2–0 win over West Ham United in the 1923 FA Cup Final. His move to Arsenal in 1928 made him the first £10,000 transfer. And their 2–0 win over Huddersfield Town in the 1930 FA Cup Final earned him the distinction of becoming the first player to win the Cup at Wembley with two different clubs.

His career record was 301 goals in 595 appearances, but as a manager he was less successful – spells at Southend United (1934–40), Middlesbrough (1944–52) and the League of Ireland side Shelbourne (1953–55) were largely unproductive. In later life he ran a greyhound track in Sunderland, took a pub in Islington and became a civil servant with the Air Ministry.

A cigarette card described him as 'a tall, elegant player with brilliant dribbling ability and deadly finishing'. He was also a chain smoker with a fabled weakness for chocolate. His childhood home at 254 Hamlet Court Road, Westcliff-on-Sea – his father Bob had been the first manager at nearby Southend – displays a Blue Plaque in his memory.

JACKSON, ELPHINSTONE, who was born the son of a High Court judge in Calcutta, India, on October 9, 1868, died in December 1945, aged 77. While at Oxford University he assisted the Corinthians and won his solitary cap for England (1891). The

Athletic News said of his performance: 'A very good back but cannot head.' After his studies he returned to Calcutta, where together with others he founded the Indian Football Association in 1893. The first recorded match in India had been at Fort William Esplanade, in Calcutta, in April 1858, when the Calcutta Club of Civilians entertained the Gentlemen of Barrackpore.

JACKSON, JOHN, the goalkeeper who appeared eight times for Scotland (1931–36) while with Partick Thistle and Chelsea, and ended his career with Guildford City, died on June 12, 1965, aged 58. Born in Glasgow on November 29, 1906, and given the nickname 'Jakey', he shared a passion for golf with many a fellow Scot and footballer, but earns a place in football's gallery of oddities for the rare distinction of demonstrating an aptitude on the links at least the equal of that he displayed on the soccer field.

As a goalkeeper he was described as 'not the biggest, but one of the most brilliant, showing superb anticipation and clean and assured handling', although on occasions luck failed him – in the Stade de Charmilles in May 1931 he was unable to keep the Swiss at bay as Scotland fell 3–2, and playing for Chelsea against Liverpool at Anfield in April 1935 he was beaten six times without reply, although on that occasion he had 'risked a bad back'. He made 49 League appearances for Chelsea in six seasons, the presence of England keeper Vic Woodley often condemning Jackson to the reserves, and during World War Two he guested for Brentford and Portsmouth.

As a golfer he was good enough to play in the 1950 British Open and was for ten years prior to his death a professional in Nova Scotia, where he died. In the 1970s many an aspiring young keeper coveted a pair of 'John Jackson Goalkeeping Gloves' – alas, the merchandise was not a belated tribute to 'Jakey', but to the Crystal Palace and Orient player known as 'Stonewall'.

JOHNSTON, JOHN LAWSON, was born in Roslin, Scotland, on
September 28, 1839, and died in Cannes, France, on November 24,
1900. As a young man he became a butcher in Edinburgh and
later left his lasting mark on football culture through his invention
in 1886 of the beef-extract drink Bovril. Although created initially
to sustain foot soldiers through harsh winter campaigns, it soon
proved an enduring terrace favourite which eventually became synonymous with the game's clichéd wintry image.

No FA Cup Final programme was complete without an
advert – 'Bovril does you the power of good', 'Bovril users are millions strong' – and top players were paid to endorse the product.
The England international Jimmy Greaves, who in later life made
public his chronic alcoholism, had earlier insisted that 'I train and
win on Bovril right through the season.' Every football ground
purveyed cups without number, and at Rangers' Ibrox Stadium
one side of the ground became known as the Bovril Stand because
of the large advert on its roof.

The warming drink made its teetotal inventor a rich man – he
sold the company in 1896 for £2 million, and his home Kingswood
House, in Southwark, was so lavishly appointed that it became
known as 'Bovril Castle'. His death aged 61 occurred aboard his
yacht *White Ladye* on the French Riviera, and he was buried in
West Norwood Cemetery, London. The resonant advertising
slogan 'Bovril puts beef into you' survived him, as did his wife and
13 children.

JONES, DAVID, the famous left full-back for Bolton Wanderers and
Manchester City, who won 14 caps for Wales between 1888 and
1900, died at Bolton on August 27, 1902, ten days after sustaining
what had appeared to be an innocuous injury while playing for
Manchester City in a practice match.

Born in Trefonen near Oswestry in 1867, he first came to
prominence with Chirk, the North Wales mining village dubbed

'the cradle of Welsh football'. Dai Jones (known as 'Di') was said to be a typical product of the club – 'preferring to use skill and judgement rather than rely on an exclusively physical approach' – a propensity being lyrically borne out by the player himself when he said that the England forward Steve Bloomer (q.v.) was 'such a beautiful player it's a shame to go for him'.

After briefly joining Newton Heath – later to become Manchester United – Jones signed for Bolton Wanderers when the Football League began in 1888. He became captain and played 228 League games in his ten-year stay – his benefit match against Everton in September 1895 marked the opening of Burnden Park.

After signing for Manchester City (1898) on the recommendation of their celebrated Welsh international Billy Meredith, a native of Chirk, Jones played 114 more League games before falling on a piece of glass and sustaining a cut knee – the wound was merely stitched, tetanus set in, and Di Jones became one of several players of the pre-war age so to perish. He was 35.

JONES, JOHN, who was capped three times at half-back for Wales in 1883–84 while with the Llangollen club Berwyn Rangers, was found shot dead in a field on his farm at Trevor, Llangollen, in the early morning of March 25, 1902. Born nearby in 1860, his playing career spanned the years 1878 to 1889. Considered 'a gritty and tireless worker' at Berwyn, noted pioneers of Welsh football, he also served Denbigh, Vale of Llangollen and Ruthin. The manner of his death alone has assured that his name yet arouses macabre curiosity. An inquest concluded that 'there was nothing to indicate whether he had taken his own life or whether an accident had taken place'. One suggestion was that the gun could have discharged when he was climbing over a gate. He was one of five players named John Jones born in the reign of Victoria to play for Wales – the other four survived him but Her Majesty did not.

JONES, JOHN LEONARD, the revered Welsh international half-back, died in Sunderland on November 24, 1931, aged 67. Playing for Southern League Tottenham Hotspur in the 1901 FA Cup Final, he became the first man in the era of League football to captain a non-League side to FA Cup victory. The feat has never been emulated since, nor is it likely to be.

Spurs' first international player, his 132 appearances (1897–1904) heralded their entry into the Football League in 1908. His career had by then ended via a short-lived excursion with an exhibition side which staged matches on an indoor 'turf carpet' at Olympia.

Described as 'most capable, speedy on the ball, clever but not showy, and passing nicely at every opportunity', 'Jack' Jones retired from football to become a cricket professional with Leinster (1907) and later took a similar engagement with a club in Durban, South Africa. He was afterwards employed as a pattern maker, and it was while so engaged that the former Spurs hero met his death, falling down a 12-foot stairway at work and sustaining head injuries which proved fatal. For posterity he left his book *Association Football – a Treatise on the Game* (1904), one of the earliest instructional works in soccer's canon.

JOY, BERNARD, an England defender, also a schoolteacher, and later football correspondent for the *Evening Standard* and *Sunday Express*, died aged 72 on July 18, 1984. His place in the record books – unlikely to be superseded – is as the last man to play for England without remuneration. Born in Fulham on October 29, 1911, he graduated from London University and began playing for the celebrated amateur club Casuals, leading them to victory over Ilford in the 1936 FA Amateur Cup Final. While still registered with Casuals he joined Arsenal, making 89 League appearances between 1935 and 1946.

His sole full England cap was gained in a 3–2 away defeat to

Belgium on May 9, 1936, making him the last amateur – literally 'a lover' of the game – to play for the national side. He also won ten caps for the England amateur side and was captain of the Great Britain football team at the 1936 Olympics in Berlin. During World War Two he served in the Royal Air Force. A vocation for teaching is evidenced through his books *Improve your Soccer* (1949) and *Play Better Football* (1951). His further work *Forward Arsenal* (1952) was one of the earliest histories of the club.

KENRICK, JARVIS, who occupies an unassailable and romantic place in the annals of association football, died at Meads Cottage, 39 Westdown Road, Blatchington, Sussex, on January 29, 1949. He was the first player to score a goal in the Football Association Challenge Cup competition (the 'FA Cup'), which feat he performed for Clapham Rovers away to Upton Park in the inaugural First Round games played on November 11, 1871, after 15 minutes' play. Kenrick later won the Cup three times running with Wanderers (1876–78). He was a left-sided attacker of whom Alcock's *Football Annual* observed: 'fair down a side, rather slack at times, but generally near the goal when the ball is there'. Kenrick played once for England – the 1872 pre-official international against Scotland – and in an 1875 encounter against Queen's Park in Glasgow was sufficiently bold to play for Wanderers in a fetching cap of 'cerise and French grey'.

A Lancing College old boy, by profession a solicitor, he played one game of cricket for Surrey (1876). He was born at Chichester, Sussex, on November 13, 1852, the date affording him another record, for when he died aged 96 years and 77 days, with the knowledge that Matt Busby's Manchester United had won the 1948 FA Cup, he was the last member of the great Wanderers side to pass away and the oldest link with the earliest days of competitive football. Not a single soul who survived him had enjoyed a longer first-hand experience of the game.

KENYON-SLANEY, COL. RT. HON. WILLIAM SLANEY, the scorer at one minute past three on Saturday March 8, 1873 of the England team's first ever goal – also the first in any international football match – died at his home Hatton Grange, Shifnal, Shropshire, on April 24, 1908. His unassailable feat occurred in the 4–2 victory against Scotland at the Kennington Oval in his sole appearance for his country, only the second official international game and the first ever held in England. He claimed his second goal after 60 minutes.

He was born in Rajkot, Gujarat, India, on August 24, 1847. After attending Eton College and Christ Church, Oxford, he had an illustrious military career, serving in the Grenadier Guards and seeing active service in the Egyptian campaign (1882), where his exertions in the Battle of Tel-el-Kebir earned him a campaign medal and the Khedive's Star. He then entered politics and was Conservative MP for Newport, Shropshire (1888–1908), and a Privy Councillor from 1904.

Kenyon-Slaney's sporting prowess – as 'a dashing lively attacker' – led to him appearing in three FA Cup Finals, winning with the Wanderers (1873) and being twice runner-up with Old Etonians. To celebrate his marriage to Lady Mabel Selina Bridgeman in 1887, Aston Villa played an exhibition match against Shifnal FC, of which he was president. Such a tribute is thought to be unique in the game's history. He was besides a well-known cricketer, playing 11 games for M.C.C. (1869–80) at an average of 10.35.

He was vice-president of the Shropshire Chess Association (1894) and in 1908 was made president of the Severnside Bowling Club, Shrewsbury, but died soon afterwards, aged 60 – as a mark of respect the post was left unfilled for the remainder of the season. He owned about 4,000 acres and his death followed an attack of gout.

Kerins, Andrew, born in the village of Ballymote, County Sligo, Ireland, on May 18, 1840, died at Dumfries, Scotland, on April 17, 1915, aged 74, having made a mark in football greater than any he ever intended. On joining the Marist Order at the age of 24 he adopted the religious name Brother Walfrid and became a teacher. In the 1870s he left Ireland for Glasgow, where on November 6,

1887 he founded a football club, his intention being to raise money and create a sense of community amongst Irish Catholic immigrants in the city's East End. Among names considered were Erin, Shamrock, Emerald and Glasgow Hibernian, but Walfrid's own preference prevailed and the resultant Celtic Football Club became one of the greatest institutions in the world game.

Brother Walfrid was in 1893 sent by his religious order to London's East End, where he continued to employ football for benevolent means by organising matches for the barefoot children in the districts of Bethnal Green and Bow. He later suffered ill health and was transferred to Mount St Michael's retirement home in Dumfries, where he died and is buried.

He remained respected and revered throughout Glasgow for his charitable works and devotion to the poor, and on November 5, 2005, a commemorative sculpture of 'the founder of Celtic' was unveiled outside the club's Celtic Park stadium. Brother Walfrid was said by contemporaries to be 'a man of enormous drive and vision'. He was fluent in French.

KIFFORD, JOHN, late West Bromwich Albion full-back, died at Paisley, Scotland, on November 21, 1921, aged 42. After a lifetime spent entertaining the public in one way or another, he deserved a more fitting end.

In 1907, after 96 League games and eight goals for the 'Throstles' – plus six appearances for Derby County – he threw in his lot with the Fred Karno 'Fun Factory' comedy troupe, touring United States theatres with fellow hopefuls Charles 'Charlie' Chaplin and Arthur Stanley Jefferson – later 'Stan Laurel' – comedy partner to Oliver Hardy.

The experience had a debilitating effect on 'Jackie' Kifford, for he died 'of unsound mind' – one of few footballers ever so labelled – in the Paisley Asylum for the General Paralysis of the Insane. He also played a number of times for Millwall.

KING, CHARLES JAMES STUART, whose regal name graced the Oxford University rearguard in their 1880 FA Cup Final defeat to Clapham Rovers, died aged 67 on April 23, 1928, at Chardstock, Devon, where he managed the National School. When King won his blue at Oxford (1881) a contemporary commented: 'A powerful back, kicks with great vigour, but a little erratic at times' – doubtless a thinly veiled reference to his terrible Cup Final miskick which a year earlier had allowed Lloyd-Jones to score the only goal of the match for Clapham Rovers close to the call of time. According to *The Sportsman* this led to 'vociferous cheering, throwing up of hats, and other demonstrations of delight', while the distraught King was for ever burdened with the painful memory of the first truly head-clutching bloomer in Cup Final history.

He was a schoolmaster, spending some years in the United States before retiring to the West Country, and was born at New Road Rectory, Leigh-on-Sea, Essex, on June 2, 1860. After his death his son presented Chardstock School with a stuffed owl in memory of his father, who had shot it in Minnesota.

KINNAIRD, LORD ARTHUR 'ALFRED' FITZGERALD, KT, who stood pre-eminent in the world of association football, died aged 75 on January 30, 1923. His spirits had been low since the death of his wife Mary 11 days earlier. Born to an old Perth family on February 16, 1847, at 35 Hyde Park Gardens, Kensington, his long playing career (spanning the 1860s to the 1890s) embraced nine FA Cup Finals – six with Old Etonians and three with Wanderers – and his record of five winner's medals has never been surpassed. Kinnaird celebrated the fifth in 1882 by standing on his head in front of the Oval pavilion.

A lofty figure and auburn beard distinguished him no less than his trademark playing outfit – long white flannels, whatever jersey was necessary, and a blue and white quartered cricket cap. He filled every position including goalkeeper, donating his services liberally – during 1867–68 he played for Kent, Cambridge University, the Wanderers, Trinity College, Old Etonians, Old Harrovians, Civil Service and Avengers. Also he captained Eton and Harrow against the World.

After one game a critic stated that 'the fleet-footed Kinnaird was here, there and everywhere', a phrase later crudely adapted into a terrace chant. He was a proponent of 'hacking', and when his wife expressed to a friend the fear that he might one day suffer a broken leg, she was knowingly assured: 'Pray do not be alarmed. If anybody's leg is broken, it will not be Arthur's.' Lord Kinnaird won one full cap for Scotland (1873) and played with vigorous enthusiasm well into his forties.

His proficiency extended to many sports – he was a real tennis blue, fives player and swimmer at Cambridge, and when at Eton the winner of an international canoe race at the Paris Exhibition of 1867. He was also a fine sprinter and a member of M.C.C.

'Alfred' Kinnaird served football as an administrator for 54 years. In 1869 he became an FA committee man at the age of 22, was treasurer between 1878 and 1890, and finally president from 1890 until 1923. He also took a prominent part in the House of Lords, and his main business interest was as a director of Barclays Bank. He was besides a philanthropist and evangelical churchman, who once said of football: 'I believe that all right-minded people have good reason to thank God for the great progress of this popular national game.'

His end came at his home – 10 St James's Square, Westminster – where three British Prime Ministers had lived before him. Each occupant bar Kinnaird is honoured by the Blue Plaque which adorns the property. He is buried at the family estate of Rossie Priory, Inchture, Perthshire.

KIPLING, JOSEPH RUDYARD, the celebrated British author born in Bombay, India, on December 30, 1865, died from a cerebral haemorrhage at his home in Burwash, East Sussex, on January 18, 1936. Of football talent he had none – at school his eyesight was said to be too poor for him to excel at sports – and he was therefore inclined towards contempt in the matter of ball games.

Over a century after his 'muddied oafs at the goals' jibe appeared in *The Islanders* (1903) it is regularly invoked by football's more pompous critics to discredit the association game – this despite Kipling actually having in mind the hybrid oddities which he had seen played at the great public schools.

His obituary is further earned for his celebrated poem 'If', containing the line: 'If you can meet with triumph and disaster and treat those two impostors just the same' – which afforded him an unlikely entry into the football dressing room. The verse was first linked to football when it was recited by Desmond Lynam during the 1998 World Cup – and subsequently recorded by him – but the apogee was reached in December 2006 when Luton Town manager Mike Newell acquainted his players with the poem after they had suffered eight League defeats in a row. Whilst a *Daily Telegraph* reporter remained sceptical – 'the players probably think Kipling makes cakes' – Luton ended their dismal run with a 2–0 triumph over League leaders Preston.

Players have not always responded so positively. A decade earlier the Rangers and Scotland goalkeeper Andy Goram – both a 'flannelled fool' and 'muddied oaf' since he also played cricket for Scotland – chided the poet for words not in fact his own: 'See the boy Rudyard Kipling, who said it wasn't whether you won or lost but how you played the game, well he obviously never played football. Winning is the only thing that matters.'

The boy Kipling was 70 at his death, and later acquired an unlikely link with David and Victoria Beckham, for like two of their children Brooklyn and Romeo his name is owed to geography, his parents having enjoyed an idyllic part of their courtship at Rudyard Lake in Staffordshire, prior to their removal to India.

LAMB, TOBY (THE), much-petted mascot of Morton Football Club, having been granted the freedom of Cappielow Park, drowned in the club bath in 'circumstances unknown' part-way through the Scottish League Division One programme for 1910–11.

Toby's special place in the Lanarkshire club had been secured after the team's centre-forward Tommy Gracie (q.v.) – son of a master butcher – struck up a generous sponsorship deal with a local trader who promised the club a lamb each time they scored during 1910–11. No sooner were the goals dispatched than the lambs (already butchered) followed, but Glasgow-born Gracie – described as 'an intelligent, good-humoured, modest young man' – took pity on Toby and saved the creature from the knife in favour of 'lucky-charm' duties.

Soon after Toby's fatal early bath, his erstwhile master was transferred to Everton, and before long he too perished in tragic circumstances.

LANGTON, HAROLD, widely known as 'Harry', a former London sports journalist and inveterate collector of football memorabilia, died of a heart attack on September 6, 2000, having earlier struck a deal which preserved for posterity football's most valued legacy. His half-century accumulation of 4,000 football artefacts – the 'Langton Collection' – today forms a key part of the historically important holdings of the National Football Museum in Preston.

Langton loved the game in a way some would regard as child-like or overly sentimental. He found in workaday objects – ceramics, toys, artwork, books, programmes and the like – both an inherent beauty and the very spirit of the game itself. These he collected for purely aesthetic reasons, concerned neither with monetary worth or their value as social history. His collection began in the 1950s when his wife Ann bought him a five-shilling print as a gift – Harry was later to say that 'from there it rather got out of hand'.

One of his most prized items was the world's first ever football book – *Discorso Sopra Il Giuoco Del Calcio*, published in Florence in 1580 – but that this should sit alongside his own more modest work *Arsenal, Arsenal!* (1971) illustrates the eclectic nature of his holdings. A number of years prior to his death his collection had been languishing in the attic of his London home, and he died shortly before it went on show. Although 'The Father of Football Memorabilia' was little known in the game's most worldly circles, his passing was noted with sadness by kindred spirits everywhere.

LEA, ARTHUR, the Welsh international forward and captain of Wrexham when they won the Welsh Cup in 1893, died at Marchwiel on March 23, 1945, aged 78, where he had latterly been the landlord of the Wrest Hotel. Born in Wrexham on November 23, 1866, six years in advance of the club itself, he became a folk-loric figure in their rise and progress, serving as a player (1883–94) and later secretary.

By such deeds Lea become well-known in the Wrexham hinterland, but heightened curiosity attached itself to his name on account of the player possessing but a single arm. For appearing in exhibition games he was paid in inverse proportion to his complement of limbs, receiving ten shillings a game instead of the five shillings a week he was paid as a professional.

Remarkably his Wrexham team-mate James Roberts also had only one arm. Nor was Lea the first Welsh international thus afflicted – in 1882 Charles Frederick Ketley won his sole cap unhindered by having lost an arm in an accident at work, and lifted the Welsh Cup three times running with Druids.

Arthur Lea endured a near-tragedy in 1893 when at the age of 27 he fell seriously ill. At one point he was threatened with the loss of a leg, but came through the crisis intact. He began playing again in 1893–94 but his career ended in sad circumstances – after a victory against Druids in a Charity Cup final the Wrexham players were attacked by opposition spectators and Lea declared, 'If that's football, that's it for me.' It was his last professional appearance.

He continued his work as a postman and played cricket for Wrexham, mostly as a bowler but making several half-centuries with the bat. After his death the Arthurian legend was on occasion embellished, some sources improbably suggesting that Lea played in goal. But as the England international Kevin Keegan was once said to have observed: 'You can't play with a one-armed goalkeeper – not at this level.'

LEARY, STUART EDWARD, an accomplished centre-forward and talented county cricketer, born in Cape Town on April 30, 1933, was one of the finest all-round sportsmen to emerge from South Africa. His suicide in his home town on August 23, 1988 was as spectacular as it was tragic. After riding the cable car to the summit of Table Mountain he dined alone in the plateau-top restaurant before throwing himself over the edge. He was 55 years of age.

In a ten-year spell at Charlton Athletic (1951–61) he scored 153 goals in 376 games and became an idol of the crowd. Cricketer Colin Cowdrey likened him to George Best – although this was an overstatement, Leary was good enough to win an England under-23 cap, and failed to win full honours only because he was declared ineligible on grounds of nationality. He ended his career at Queen's Park Rangers, still scoring regularly. As a cricketer he made 16,169 runs for Kent (1951–71) and took 140 wickets and 362 catches.

Although popular with his male colleagues he was said by one to be 'somewhat camp', rather 'too fond of the comb', and 'inclined to self-mocking homosexual nuances'. In the Kent team photographs for 1969 and 1970 he jokingly placed his hand on a colleague's knee, and in football was one of the first players to endure terrace taunts about his sexuality, it being recorded that his selection when off-form was sometimes crudely questioned: 'Leary, you must be having an affair with the manager.'

Shortly before killing himself he had faced a depressive illness which caused spectacular mood swings. There were rumours that he had suffered big losses in gold-mining investments. Several close friends revealed that he feared he may be infected by the deadly AIDS virus, and was particularly apprehensive about a national investigation into juvenile vice. He had been married but divorced, and went to the grave an enigma. When quizzed about Leary's personal life, a former colleague said, 'He had about five girlfriends on the go at the time of his death.'

LENNON, JOHN WINSTON, a founder member of the Beatles pop group, was shot dead by a crazed fan outside his New York apartment on December 8, 1980, aged 40. Since his birthplace was Liverpool (October 9, 1940) it has been thought incongruous that he failed to acquire even a passing interest in football, save perhaps as a schoolboy. His dogged refusal to declare an allegiance to either Liverpool or Everton was born of a sublime indifference to the game, a sentiment common to the Beatles as a whole. George Harrison's reply to those impertinent enough to ask which club he supported was: 'There are three teams in Liverpool and I prefer the other one' – while Paul McCartney declared: 'We all support Liverpool and Everton – I know it's not allowed, but never mind.'

In common with Gary Winston Lineker his middle name paid homage to Winston Churchill, but his football obituary is earned for two artistic legacies. A childhood football picture executed by Lennon in June 1952 was used on the album cover for *Walls and Bridges* (1974) – even then the 11-year-old chose not to draw

Liverpool and Everton, but depicted instead that year's FA Cup finalists Arsenal and Newcastle United, with Newcastle's winning number nine Jackie Milburn shown centre-stage. Lennon's second nod to the game is a typically surreal pun from his book *In His Own Write* (1964): 'Anything you say may be used in Everton against you.'

LEWIS, DANIEL, the Wales and Arsenal goalkeeper, whose infamous fumble in the 1927 FA Cup Final against Cardiff City permitted a Welsh club to win the trophy for the first and only time, died on July 17, 1965, aged 62.

Dan Lewis made his Arsenal debut in 1924, having earlier learned his craft with the Welsh club Mardy. Although he played 142 League games for the Gunners he is remembered for his sole FA Cup Final appearance, at Wembley Stadium on April 23, 1927. After 75 minutes the Cardiff striker Hughie Ferguson (q.v.) prodded a tame shot towards goal. Lewis dropped down to make what appeared to be a comfortable save, momentarily clutching the ball securely to his chest before inexplicably allowing it to squirm from his grasp into the net. No further goals being registered, the Welsh nation collectively celebrated as the Cup left England for the first and only time, while a crestfallen Arsenal missed their opportunity to gain a first major trophy.

Lewis compounded his error by advancing a legendary excuse, suggesting the shiny surface of his new jersey had caused the ball to slither through the crook of his elbow. When Arsenal next reached the Cup Final in 1930 – against Huddersfield Town – Lewis was nursing an injury and was conveniently replaced by the Indian-born keeper Charlie Preedy. Ironically, Preedy made a string of dreadful errors without being punished, and the newly christened 'Lucky Arsenal' emerged 2–0 victors. Lewis's faith in justice was severely diminished, and he was sold to Gillingham in January 1931, where he played only six League games before retiring.

He was born in Mardy, Glamorgan, on December 11, 1902, and played three times for Wales. With the passing years he became accustomed to his place in football's 'Hall of Shame' and was enjoying a carefree summer holiday in Scarborough when his life ended suddenly. He was survived by film footage of his fateful error now widely viewed on the internet for idle amusement.

LIDDELL, WILLIAM BEVERIDGE, the Liverpool footballer, considered by many the finest player ever to represent the club, died aged 79 of Alzheimer's disease on July 3, 2001, survived by his wife and two sons. Born at Townhill, near Dunfermline, on January 10, 1922 – the eldest of six children of a coal miner who was determined that Billy would not go down the pits – he signed professional for Liverpool in 1939 after being spotted playing for Lochgelly Violet by the Liverpool wing-half Matt Busby.

War service as a Bomber Command pilot officer and pathfinder prevented him making his full League debut until 1946, but his impact was immediate – Liverpool won the 1946–47 League Championship, their first in 24 years, with the free-scoring centre-forward Albert Stubbins (q.v.) reaping great benefit from Liddell's unerring supply.

Liddell won 28 Scottish caps (1947–56) and when he retired in 1961 had played 537 times for Liverpool – his only first-class club – and scored 229 goals. Known as 'King Billy' or 'William the Conqueror', his loyalty knew no bounds, and he was so esteemed that in his heyday the team was dubbed 'Liddellpool'.

Chiefly a raiding outside-left, but adept at centre-forward, his attributes were a lightning speed and fearsome strength which rendered him a torment even to the best defenders. But withal he was supremely modest and considered a model pro – hard but fair, a committed Christian, Sunday school teacher and lay preacher, who worked as an accountant throughout his football career. In 1958 he was appointed a JP, and when he finished playing became assistant bursar at Liverpool University, continuing to watch Liverpool as a season ticket holder.

A staunch teetotaller, he was described by Brian Glanville in his *Guardian* obituary as 'the perfect sportsman, almost too good to be true', a sentiment also reflected in the mischievous gift given to Liddell when he broke the Liverpool appearance record – he was presented by the club with a cocktail cabinet.

LIPTON, SIR THOMAS JOHNSTONE, BT, KCVO, the self-made millionaire grocery baron, who was born to poor Irish parents in Glasgow, Scotland on May 10, 1850, died on October 2, 1931, his name having become established in the English vernacular through his famous Lipton tea brand.

As a sportsman he was most closely associated with yachting – on five occasions between 1899 and 1930 challenging without success the American holders of the Americas Cup with his yachts called *Shamrock* – but his great vision and generosity also made possible one of the most romantic episodes in football history.

In 1909 at the behest of Italian business acquaintances the grocery baron organised the first 'world football tournament' – held in Turin, Italy, it has been informally dubbed 'the first World Cup'. Due to FA restrictions Lipton was obliged to send an amateur team to represent Britain – the honour fell to the lowly County Durham side West Auckland Town, who in the final on April 12, 1909 overcame FC Winterthur of Switzerland to lift the massive, solid silver Sir Thomas Lipton Trophy. Buoyed by the success of his brainchild, Lipton repeated the event in 1911, when West Auckland again emerged victorious, this time inflicting a humbling 6–1 defeat on Juventus in the final.

The remarkable story was dramatised in the 1982 Tyne Tees Television film *A Captain's Tale*, some artistic licence being employed in the sequence of events. Lipton's tournament was never staged again, but its success was quietly noted by the fledgling administrative body for world football, and in 1930 the FIFA World Cup was inaugurated.

To Sir Thomas Lipton must go some of the credit, and he lived to know that Uruguay had become the first official World Champions. When he died aged 81 he left no issue, having remained a lifelong bachelor who once dryly quipped that 'my only blood relatives are some New Jersey mosquitoes'. At his death he was the oldest Freemason on the membership roll of Lodge Scotia No. 178 in Glasgow.

LOGAN, JAMES, who died unexpectedly on May 25, 1896, was only the second player to score a hat-trick in an FA Cup Final – for Notts County in their 4–1 defeat of Bolton Wanderers in 1894. He became an instant hero at Notts but his career embraced a further six clubs in both England and Scotland. He won his sole Scottish cap in 1891.

Jimmy Logan was playing for Loughborough Town when his death occurred. On April 4, 1896, in a Second Division match at Newton Heath (later Manchester United), the Luffs XI turned out in ordinary clothes when the team strip was forgotten. After it rained heavily during their 2–0 defeat Logan caught a chill through travelling home still wearing his sodden outfit. He recovered to play another game but suffered a relapse and died of pneumonia. Born in Troon on June 24, 1870, he was 25 when the tragedy occurred. Loughborough Town survived him – reaching their zenith in an 8–0 defeat of Woolwich Arsenal – but disappeared from the League in 1900.

LOWRY, LAURENCE STEPHEN, who died of pneumonia at The Woods Hospital, Glossop, Derbyshire, aged 88, on February 23, 1976, was a renowned English artist who through his work secured himself an unlikely place in the cultural landscape of British football.

He was born on November 1, 1887 in Stretford, Manchester, not far from the site of what would later become Old Trafford, the world-famous home ground of Manchester United. His mother Elizabeth was barely able to look at him for some time after the birth without undisguised distaste – she had desperately desired a girl – expressing her envy of her sister Mary who had 'three splendid daughters' instead of 'one clumsy boy'.

His most celebrated work – *Going to the Match* – depicts eager spectators converging on Burnden Park, then the home ground of Bolton Wanderers. Lowry entered the canvas in the 1953 exhibition *Football and the Fine Arts*, organised to celebrate the 90th anniversary of the Football Association, and won first prize. In December 1999 the game reclaimed the picture when the Professional Footballers' Association bought it at a Sotheby's sale in London for £1.9 million – a record auction price for a modern British painting – against an estimate of £500,000. PFA Chief Executive Gordon Taylor, widely criticised for his apparent profligacy, said: 'I desperately wanted the painting because it represents the heart and soul of the game and the anticipation of fans on their way to a match.' Taylor was a former Bolton Wanderers winger.

Known for his eccentricity – always well wrapped up even in warm weather – Lowry never married and claimed never to have had a girlfriend, saying that he lived only for his mother's approval, which he never fully won. He neither drank alcohol nor smoked and the collection of clocks in his living room were all set at different times. Society sought to honour him, but he refused an OBE in 1955, a CBE in 1961, a Knighthood in 1968, and Orders of the Companion of Honour in 1972 and 1976 – a record for the most honours declined.

In 2005 a statue of the artist was unveiled in Mottram, Tameside, close to The Elms in Stalybridge Road, the house in which Lowry lived from 1948 until his death. L.S. Lowry is buried in Chorlton Southern Cemetery, Manchester, where the grave of

the former Manchester United manager Sir Matt Busby may also be found.

LUBBOCK, EDGAR, England half-back, the youngest of eight great Lubbocks, all of whom excelled at sport, died at 18 Hans Court, Chelsea, on September 9, 1907. He was better known to his contemporaries as 'Quintus' because, when he arrived at Eton, four of his elder brothers were still at the school. Lubbock was praised as 'the finest kick anywhere, truly the bane of all forwards' – he won the FA Cup with both Wanderers (1872) and Old Etonians' (1879), gained four full England caps and played once at cricket for Kent (1871). He was also Master of the Blankney Foxhounds.

The Lubbocks were a family of bankers. At the time of his death aged 50 Edgar was deputy governor of the Bank of England. He was a man not to be trifled with, and the story has been related that in a match between the Old Etonians and the Wanderers at the Oval, C.W. Alcock, the latter's captain, elected to charge Lubbock off the ball. The Old Etonian's response serves as a fitting epitaph: 'By heaven, Alcock! If you do that again, I'll hack your legs off.'

LUDFORD, ROGER, a yeoman of South Mimms, Middlesex, near Potters Bar, perished between 3 and 4 p.m. on March 3, 1581, one of the first recorded victims of death associated with football, whose riotous enthusiasm and misplaced bravado were his grave undoing. The records of Middlesex Coroner's Court chronicle his sorry end:

> Nicholas Martyn and Richard Turvey were on the third instant playing with other persons at foote-ball in the place called Evanses Field at Southmyms, when the said Roger Ludford and one Simon Maltus came to the ground. Roger Ludford cried out, 'Cast hym over the

hedge,' indicating that he meant Nicholas Martyn, who replied, 'Come thou and do yt.' Thereupon Roger Ludford ran towards the ball with the intention to kick it, whereupon Nicholas Martyn with the fore-part of his right arm and Richard Turvey with his left arm struck Roger Ludford on the fore-part of the body under the breast, giving him a mortal blow of which he died within a quarter of an hour. Thus Nicholas and Richard in this manner slew said Roger.

Nicholas Martyn may be regarded as the earliest example of that breed of football enthusiast who in latter years adopted the clarion call, 'Come and have a go if you think you're hard enough.' That Roger Ludford took the bait proved his misfortune, and he appears to have been scarcely aided by his colleague Simon Maltus, contemporary accounts inferring that he fled the scene with undue haste.

LYTTELTON, RT. HON. ALFRED, the only cabinet minister to play football for England, died at 3 Devonshire Terrace, a nursing home in Marylebone, London, on July 5, 1913. He had served the cabinet as secretary of state for the Colonies (1903–05), it being said that 'he incurred much odium by sanctioning the scheme of importing Chinese coolies into Johannesburg to remedy the shortness of native labour.'

His style at football betrayed a selfish streak. In his solitary game for England – March 3, 1877, against Scotland at The Oval – he scored England's only goal in a sobering 3–1 reversal. But his persistence in playing the old-fashioned dribbling game in favour of new-style 'combination' earned him a sharp rebuke from team-mate Billy Mosforth, a Sheffield Wednesday player, to which Lyttelton gave the sneering riposte: 'I play for my own pleasure.'

That he had talent at soccer cannot be denied – 'strong and fast, perhaps the most dangerous forward out' – but his prowess at cricket earned him a record in 1880 that can never be beaten. By playing against Australia at The Oval in the first Test match to be played in England he became the first man to appear for England at both football and cricket, and the world's first double international at these sports.

Born in Westminster, London, on February 7, 1857, the eighth son of the fourth Lord Lyttelton, he was regarded by contemporaries as perhaps the most gifted all-round sportsman of his generation. At Trinity College, Cambridge he won blues for soccer, cricket, rackets, real tennis and athletics, although in 1876 he came only second in throwing the hammer. As a cricketer his final Test match against Australia (1884) earned him legendary status – although wicketkeeper, he was called upon to bowl when the Australians had amassed over 500 runs with only six wickets down. W.G. Grace deputised behind the stumps while Lyttelton employed underarm lobs to take the final four wickets for only 19 runs off 12 overs.

He was by profession a barrister, becoming a QC and later KC, and was MP for Warwick and Leamington 1895–1906 and for St George's, Hanover Square, 1906–13. He was twice married, only his second wife surviving him. Death visited him unexpectedly after he was taken ill at a Foreign Office dinner held to mark his return from holiday in Africa. It transpired he had a few days earlier been hit in the stomach by a cricket ball during an innings of 89. An operation revealed an abscess and 'a bad state of things' and he died a week later aged 56.

His loyal brother Edward (q.v.) wrote in a memoir: 'There have been other players better at dribbling, a very few of greater speed and some heavier, but I never knew one who combined the three great essentials, and added to them a surprising accuracy at kicking goals and "bunting" his opponents by dint of a jerk of the hips.

Once playing against the Royal Engineers I saw him make a run from one end of the field to the other, flooring four men on the way, then shoot a goal at the end.'

As a passionate late-life golfer he ordered his Lutyens-designed holiday home 'Greywalls' in Scotland to be built 'within a mashie niblick of the eighteenth green at Muirfield'. The great Liberal Prime Minister William Ewart Gladstone was his uncle.

LYTTELTON, THE REV. THE HON. DR EDWARD, headmaster of Eton College 1905–16, former Middlesex county cricketer and England international football player, died on January 26, 1942, aged 86. Born in Westminster on July 23, 1855, his record as a cricketer stands scrutiny – he was captain of Cambridge University, scorer in 1878 of the first century ever made against the Australians in England, amassed a run total of 2,013 for Middlesex (1878–82) and was a member of M.C.C. – but his prowess on the soccer field, where he was described by *The Sportsman* as 'a very good back, hard to pass and a strong kick', should not be overlooked.

He and his brother Alfred (q.v.) – the all-rounder *par excellence* – were in the same Old Etonians side for the drawn and replayed FA Cup Final of 1876, which ended in their 3–0 defeat by Wanderers. In his one appearance for England (1878) Edward was unable to quell the tide when they suffered a 7–2 defeat by Scotland. In the same year he gained his Classical Tripos at Cambridge prior to becoming a schoolmaster and clergyman.

When his sporting vigour declined he turned to writing. *Cricket* (1890) paid homage to his greatest passion, while in *Training of the Young in the Laws of Sex* (1900) – which became a much-relied-upon text – he urged that 'the creeping serpent of self-abuse' must be tamed at all costs.

Following the death of his wife Caroline in July 1919 (they had two daughters, Norah and Delia) he listed his solitary recreations as music and scenery. He later wrote *The Christian and Birth*

Control (1929) – a curious title, since his father the fourth Lord Lyttelton, an ardent Christian, had progeny amounting to 15 by two marriages.

At the close of his life Edward Lyttelton's home was at Grangegorman, Overstrand, Norfolk, but he died at The Old Palace, Lincoln, and is buried there. The celebrated jazz musician Humphrey Richard Adeane Lyttelton, born at Eton College in 1921, shares a common ancestry.

MADDEN, JOHN WILLIAM, a former riveter in a Glasgow shipyard, born in Dumbarton on June 11, 1865, was twice capped by Scotland (1893–95) at centre-forward, scoring five goals. His football obituary is earned via the 'most unexpected statue' category, his likeness having been erected in the Czech capital Prague, after he died there on April 17, 1948, aged 82.

Known as 'The Rooter' at his main club Celtic (1888–96), he also assisted Dumbarton and Dundee and had transient spells in England with Gainsborough Trinity and Tottenham Hotspur. One of the first in British football to venture into Europe as a coach, he managed Slavia Prague over three decades (from 1905 until the 1930s) and established the club as the leading force in Czech football.

At the 1934 World Cup Final Jock Madden became one of the few Scots in history to retain an interest in that stage of the competition, when seven of his Slavia Prague side were in the Czech team beaten by Italy. Still coaching from a wheelchair at the age of 73 he became an institution in Prague and is buried there.

MACAULAY, REGINALD HEBER, an England centre-forward, died aged 79 on December 15, 1937, in Hampstead. Born at Hodnet, Shropshire, on August 24, 1858, his athletic bent emerged at Eton and continued at Cambridge. While still a student he scored the solitary goal in the 1882 FA Cup Final which earned Old Etonians their famous victory over favourites Blackburn Rovers, the last triumph of the amateur southern gents over the upcoming industrial north.

Although selected only once for England – the 6–1 home

defeat by Scotland in 1881 – he numbers three achievements which none of his ilk can match. In 1879 he was English high-jump champion. A year later he co-founded the Amateur Athletics Association. And in his rock garden at Kirnan, Scotland – where he spent time after retiring as an East India merchant – he bred a notable addition to the gardens of modern times – *Gentiana Macaulayi*. His grave in Hampstead Church belies his talents, giving no clue to either his sporting or horticultural achievements.

MARTIN, LEONARD, a celebrated voice in British football, died on August 21, 1995, aged 76. Although seldom recognised in the street, the Australian-born broadcaster's distinctive delivery of the classified football results on the 'Final Score' section of BBC television's Saturday afternoon sports programme *Grandstand* rendered him something of a national treasure.

Len read the results from the very first broadcast, on October 11, 1958, until his death 37 years later. Lauded for 'his almost telepathic style of intonation in the delivery of a score' – in truth a skill more relevant to radio – viewers were enabled without even looking at the screen to reliably divine a 'win, lose or draw' before Martin had completed his reading. By such means he was empowered to make or break a weekend for a substantial portion of the British population.

As well as his *Grandstand* job, Leonard Martin was a voice-over artist heard on Movietone newsreels and he was the narrator of *The Long Night Haul* (1956), a documentary about the British Road Services, the celebrated UK haulage network. Such impressive credits aside, his finest hour might well have been afforded by the Scottish Division Two game played at Station Park before a crowd of 900 on April 22, 1964, which finished Forfar 5 East Fife 4. However, Martin was denied an iconic moment since the game took place on a Wednesday. He was succeeded in his role by Tim Gudgin, another master of intonation.

MCAULAY, JAMES, who died on January 13, 1943, was the first of several eminent footballers of the Victorian age awarded the epithet 'The Prince of Goalkeepers'. He was born by the River Leven in Bonhill, Dunbartonshire, on August 28, 1860, aligning himself with Dumbarton FC when they took possession of Boghill Park in 1879, whereupon a remarkable run ensued in which they did not lose a home game for five years.

He won a Scottish Cup medal with Dumbarton in 1883, yet his fame as a goalkeeper arose by chance, for he was originally an outfield player – 'as a back, kicks and tackles brilliantly, as a forward, most judicious' – and first donned the custodial jersey only because the regular goalkeeper John 'Diver' Kennedy had 'lost form'. In nine games for Scotland (1882–87) McAulay never finished on the losing side – he scored on his debut, playing at centre-forward, but thereafter retreated permanently between the sticks, his style being described as 'intrepid' and 'cool to the point of nonchalance'.

He retired from football prematurely in 1887 – sailing for Burma to pursue his profession as an engineer – yet when the nineteenth century closed he retained the distinction of being the 'longest unbeaten' international goalkeeper up to that time. On returning to Dumbarton in later years he became prominent in public life, serving as a JP and Honorary Sheriff. The original 'Prince of Goalkeepers' had attained 82 years at his death, having spent the substantial part of his working life with the Irrawaddy Steam Navigation Company.

MCBAIN, NEIL, a Scottish international wing-half linked to a plethora of clubs, died on May 13, 1974, aged 78. Described as 'composed and with a delicate touch, and magnificent at headwork', his name would yet be consigned to obscurity but for the emergency he encountered on March 15, 1947, when managing New Brighton in a Division Three (North) game at Hartlepool United.

His ranks woefully depleted, McBain was compelled to keep goal himself, thereby becoming the oldest player to appear in a Football League game, aged 51 years and 120 days, and at the same time establishing another record, a playing career exceeding 32 years. New Brighton lost 3–0, having also called upon the services of 'young Nick', the son of a Hartlepool director. Although McBain was applauded off the field and given a large whisky, the state of disarray at his club was scarcely alleviated. A year later he was sacked with New Brighton sitting bottom of the League.

Born in Campbeltown, Argyllshire, on November 15, 1895, he signed for Ayr United in 1914, moving to Manchester United in 1921 for £4,500, subsequently playing for Everton, St Johnstone, Liverpool and Watford. As a manager he also took the helm at Watford, Ayr United, Luton Town and Leyton Orient – enjoying an interlude in 1949 as coach in Argentina with Estudiantes de la Plata. A pen-picture said of him that he was 'a bit adventurous, liable to give qualms to the more cautious supporter'. As an emergency goalkeeper his height was against him, being stated as 5ft 8in in 1925, and little changed at his death.

McCRUM, WILLIAM, a Northern Irish industrialist considered the 'inventor' of the penalty kick, died aged 67 in December 1932, in the village of Milford, County Armagh, where he was born on February 7, 1865. The son of a millionaire linen magnate, he attended Armagh Royal School and Trinity College Dublin, where he proved a brilliant scholar, a fine sportsman, and a passionate advocate of 'fair play'.

While goalkeeper of Milford Everton FC he hit upon an idea aimed at punishing the growing scourge of wilfully unfair defending close to goal. In 1890 his 'penalty kick' proposal was submitted via the Irish FA to the International Football Board. Dismissively dubbed the 'Irishman's Motion', it caused a storm of protest, and only after a series of shameless fouls had occurred in key games in

England and Scotland did a change of heart occur. On June 2, 1891, the penalty kick was finally drafted into the Laws of the game.

Its creator was known in Milford as 'Master Willie', the flamboyant managing director of the family business, who alas enjoyed the high life to excess. Shunned by his wealthy father, and deserted by his wife, he sought solace on the gambling tables of Monte Carlo, where injudicious speculations hastened his ruination. He died in an Armagh boarding house – penniless, alone, and alcoholic. Only after the ritual of 'penalties' had gained later notoriety was McCrum's name raised from obscurity. In 2007 approval was given for a memorial to be erected in Milford on the very field where 'Master Willie' first tried out his brainwave.

McFARLANE, PROF. JAMES WALTER, was the leading British Scandinavian scholar of his generation, whose death aged 78 on August 9, 1999, prompted an unlikely obituary in the hallowed journal of the Association of Football Statisticians.

It bears reiteration for being illustrative of the period during the Second World War when keen amateurs of McFarlane's ilk filled the football breach alongside seasoned professionals, thereby helping to sustain national morale.

Born in Sunderland on December 12, 1920, he assisted his home-town club as a wartime centre-half, once being called upon to mark the great England centre-forward Tommy Lawton. When asked what it was like he said knowingly: 'Hard – all elbows.' Those most unequal of 'equals' on the playing pitch also lived disparate lives off it. After completing his Oxford degree in 1947 McFarlane became an inspirational figure at the University of East Anglia. When Lawton's *My Twenty Years of Soccer* was published in 1955, McFarlane's eight-volume study of the works of Henrik Ibsen was not far behind.

Professor McFarlane later founded the Norvik Press – 'specialists in all aspects of Scandinavian literature' – and retired to the idyllic village of Stody in Norfolk, where he died. In stark contrast the sale proceeds of *Tommy Lawton's All Star Football Book* (1950) proved insufficient to secure the England star's financial future. When he died of pneumonia at his modest home in Nottingham in 1996 Lawton had suffered much hardship and no little indignity.

Football fans prone to philosophical debate might consider a vexing question, 'Which man's life would one prefer to have lived?' The tacit answer is afforded by Lawton's obituary description – 'a popular legend' – a tag which eluded McFarlane both in life and in death.

McGREGOR, WILLIAM, was born in Muthill, Perthshire, on January 27, 1846, the youngest of nine children of a tailor. By his death aged 65, on December 20, 1911, in Birmingham, he had been dubbed 'The Father of League Football'. He left Scotland for Birmingham when aged 24, opening a drapery shop there with his brother Peter. Although no footballer, claiming, 'I tried it once when very young and had to take to bed for a week', he became an enthusiast and director of Aston Villa. Spurred by their progress, and adopting an idea already established in cricket, he circulated a proposal 'that ten or 12 of the most prominent clubs in England combine to arrange home and away fixtures each season'.

Interested parties met at Anderton's Hotel, Fleet Street, London, on March 23, 1888, and soon thereafter, on April 17, at the Royal Hotel, Manchester, the Football League was founded. Twelve original members subscribed to McGregor's idea, and on Saturday September 8, 1888, the first Football League fixtures were enacted. McGregor became the first Football League chairman (1888–92), its first president (1892–94), and from 1895 until his death its first Life Member.

Association Football and the Men Who Made It (1906) described him: 'A grave, thoughtful, far-seeing son of Caledonia, his bearded benevolent face something of the Father Christmas type. His wonderful urbanity, conscientious spirit, and clean record disarm hostility. All good players are his friends and all good clubs his admirers.' He was besides a staunch Liberal, ardent Methodist, and strict teetotaller. He lived to see Aston Villa win six League titles and four FA Cup Finals, leading him to pronounce: 'For brilliance and consistency, for activity in philanthropic enterprise, for astuteness of management and for general alertness, the superiors of Aston Villa cannot be found.'

He died at 70 Newhall Street, the home of his daughter Jesse and her husband Ernest Hinchley. Of the lamentable event, the League Management Committee said: 'The death of this tactful and wise counsellor, our founding father, is an irreparable loss. He has left a record and influence on the game that will make his memory honoured and revered.' As a tribute they endowed 'the William McGregor bed' to Birmingham Hospital.

McGRORY, JAMES EDWARD, was born in Glasgow on April 26, 1904, and died there on October 20, 1982, aged 78 and a Celtic legend. That his name should gain only limited currency in football's wider circles is lamentable, since Jimmy McGrory is the greatest exponent of goal-getting in the history of British football.

His 550 strikes in first-class matches is a British record, including 410 in 408 League matches, a record for the Scottish game. His eight goals for Celtic against Dunfermline Athletic in 1928 is also a Scottish record, as is his 'fastest hat-trick' achieved in three minutes against Motherwell in 1936.

He joined Celtic in 1922 and retired as a player there in 1937, only a short loan-spell at Clydebank interrupting his run. His goal ratio for Celtic was remarkable – 397 in 378 games – yet astonishingly he was capped only seven times by Scotland. He left to become manager of Kilmarnock (1937–39) but returned to manage Celtic (1945–65) before handing over the reins to Jock Stein.

Not very tall (5ft 8in), but solidly built, McGrory was blessed with speed, control, heading power, anticipation and bravery, all the attributes of the 'complete centre-forward'. He scored a disproportionate amount of his goals with his head, earning him the moniker 'Golden Crust'.

McQUEEN, MATTHEW, the Scottish football player indelibly associated with Liverpool, died on September 29, 1944, aged 81. Born on May 18, 1863 at Harthill, Lanarkshire, Scotland, he played for Leith Athletic and Heart of Midlothian before signing for Liverpool in 1892, the year of the club's inception. The following season he appeared with his brother Hugh in Liverpool's first ever Football League fixture, when they fielded ten Scots and an unlikely Englishman named McOwen. Although primarily a right-half, Matt McQueen was the original 'utility player' – he played 49 times as goalkeeper, and by his last game in 1899 had filled all but two positions in 150 matches for the Reds.

His versatility knew no bounds – in 1918 he became a director of the club, and early in 1923 was appointed 'temporary' manager, overseeing the final stages of the campaign in which Liverpool won the 1922–23 League Championship. He remained in the manager's chair for five years, a tenure not without difficulty – whilst on a scouting mission to Sheffield in 1924 McQueen was involved in a road accident and lost a leg – and in 1928 he stepped down in poor health.

Matt McQueen played twice for Scotland (1890–91) and is thought to hold a unique record in British football – being the only player to win championship medals (Second Division 1894 and 1896) as both an outfield player and a goalkeeper. An interim stint as linesman in 1904 completed one of the most versatile records in the game. At its most luxuriant, his handlebar moustache was without equal in League football.

MILLER, GERRIT SMITH, known as 'Gat', who was born in Peterborough, Madison County, New York State, on January 28, 1845, died aged 92 on March 10, 1937. In 1862, when a 17-year-old student at Dixwell Latin School in Boston, Massachusetts, he formed the Oneida Boston Football Club – the earliest in the United States to play on organised lines, and said to be the first football club established outside England. Although undoubtedly playing what later generations would call a rugby-soccer hybrid, the club's use of a round ball was deemed significant, and on the strength of written reminiscences Gat Miller was later named 'The Father of American Soccer'.

Oneida's first recorded fixture took place on Boston Common on November 7, 1863, against a team of players from Boston Latin and Boston English schools. A memoir in the *Cornell Alumni News* of November 22, 1923 says: 'Miller was president, captain and full back of the Oneida club until it disbanded in 1865 when its founder members advanced to higher education.' In 1925 a small band of surviving players erected a granite tablet on Boston Common which records that in the pioneering club's short life 'the Oneida goal was never crossed'.

After graduating from Harvard in 1869 Gerrit Smith Miller became a noted dairy farmer and political figure. When he died in 1937 his valuable legacy to the American nation was faithfully recorded in his obituaries – namely that 'in 1869 he imported from Holland three cows and a bull – Fraulein, Dowager, Crown Princess and Hollander – from which the greater part of America's two-million-strong Holstein-Friesian herd have directly descended.'

MILTON, CLEMENT 'ARTHUR', the last man to play both football and cricket for England, died at his home in Bristol on April 25, 2007, aged 79.

Born in Bedminster on March 10, 1928, Arthur Milton was a

stylish batsman who made his debut for Gloucestershire in 1948 and was an ever-present until he retired aged 46 at the end of 1974. He made 32,150 runs for the county, took 79 wickets, and played six Test matches for England.

His football career was shorter and less spectacular. His one appearance for England was in a 2–2 draw with Austria in 1952. As a fleet-footed winger with Arsenal (1950–55) he scored 18 goals in 75 League games, and ended his career with 14 appearances for Bristol City in 1954–55. In retirement he became a postman in the Cotswolds, maintaining his fitness by jumping on and off his bicycle during his rounds. His death occurred on the same day as that of fellow Arsenal player Alan Ball (q.v.) and was rather overshadowed by it. In all probability Milton's record will survive him forever – the last Englishman of the authentic 'double breed'.

MILTON, STANLEY, a 1930s goalkeeper whose death has never been recorded by the Football League, receives a presumptive obituary. Born in Dewsbury, West Yorkshire, in 1913, the year proved sadly prophetic. He joined Halifax Town in 1932 and made his Football League debut in a Third Division (North) game at Stockport County on January 6, 1934. No debut has been so harrowing. Reports say Milton had 'kept Halifax in it' when they trailed 2–0 at half-time, but after the break 'his confidence visibly drained'. County ran riot against 'an out-of-sorts Town team' who were eventually beaten 13–0. The score stands as the biggest victory – and defeat – in the Football League, equalled only by Newcastle United who beat Newport County by the same score in 1946. Stan Milton did not appear again that season but later played seven further games for Halifax of which six ended in defeat. Remarkably the club were able to sell him – he played nine games for York City before retiring in 1938 to blessed obscurity.

MITCHELL, JAMES FREDERICK, an England international goalkeeper who from 1914 to 1925 played 125 League games for Blackpool, Preston North End and Manchester City, died on May 30, 1975, aged 77. Born in Manchester on November 18, 1897, he was famed not only for his massive clearances and impressive stature but also because he played wearing spectacles. In his sole England appearance – a 3–1 victory against Northern Ireland in 1924 – he became the first and last England player to perform in glasses.

He turned out similarly accoutred for Preston North End in their 1922 FA Cup Final defeat by Huddersfield Town. The only goal was a controversial penalty of which the *Sunday Chronicle* said: 'Mitchell decided on the manoeuvre of dervish leaps in the air while the act was brewing, the intention obviously being to put the Huddersfield marksman off his shot.'

Mitchell was goalkeeper for England at the 1920 Olympics when they suffered a shock first-round defeat to Norway. He won six amateur international caps and remained an unpaid practitioner throughout his League career – for a time he was a master at his *alma mater* Arnold Grammar School in Blackpool, and later joined the footwear chain Stead and Simpson. His father 'Billy' Mitchell was a crack exponent at billiards who in the 1890s was several times English champion.

MOORE, BRIAN, the broadcaster known as 'The Voice of ITV Sport', died aged 69 at his home in Kent on September 1, 2001, missing England's 5–1 defeat of Germany in Munich by a matter of hours. Born in Gillingham on February 28, 1932, he initially joined the BBC as a radio reporter (1961) and was their first football correspondent, but after moving to London Weekend Television (1967) he became synonymous with ITV football over three decades.

His presentation of *The Big Match* and *On the Ball* will endure in the memory alongside his commentating gaffes – in 1980 he told 13 million viewers 'Hamburg have won the European Cup' as the

Nottingham Forest captain John McGovern hoisted the trophy aloft. His most oft-quoted line is from the Liverpool v. Arsenal 1989 Championship decider – 'it's up for grabs now' – closely followed by 'If you can't stand the heat in the dressing room get out of the kitchen.'

Known in football as 'Mooro' he was a fan and director of Gillingham FC. The club fanzine *Brian Moore's Head Looks Uncannily Like London Planetarium* was named in his honour – a line from 'Dickie Davies' Eyes' by the band Half Man Half Biscuit. He had a little-publicised passion for cricket, and at his death had been married to his wife Betty since 1955.

MORLEY, EBENEZER COBB, known as 'The Father of Association Football', died aged 93 on November 20, 1924, at Barnes, Middlesex. His end came at 26 The Terrace, where he had lived since 1862. Born in Hull on August 16, 1831, Morley became a solicitor. He moved to Barnes in 1858, and in 1862 founded Barnes FC. As club captain he wrote to *Bell's Life* newspaper proposing a universal set of rules for football. This led to the celebrated meeting at The Freemasons' Tavern in London that created the Football Association in 1863. From his home Morley drafted the first Laws of the game, and became the FA's first secretary (1863–66) and its second president (1867–74). Of the inaugural 'association football' match *The Field* newspaper said: 'It was characterised by great good temper, the rules being so simple and easy of observance that it was difficult for disputes to arise.'

As an oarsman Morley founded the Barnes and Mortlake Regatta. He also kept a pack of beagles and hunted with the Surrey Union Foxhounds. Although described as 'a vigorous athlete', his marriage to Frances Bigwood produced no issue, and in his convoluted will he left £200 to his gardener. The Father of Association Football is buried in a simple grave in Barnes Old Cemetery, and it has been pointedly remarked upon by enthusiasts that his former home has not yet been adorned by a plaque to mark his far-reaching contribution to the world's greatest game.

MORLEY, HERBERT, born at Kiveton Park, Sheffield, in October 1882, died aged 74 on July 15, 1957. A pen-picture labelled him 'a fearless right-back whose renowned dash is in no way lessened by a particularly large physique.' In 93 League games for Grimsby Town (1904–06) and 258 for Notts County (1906–14) he honed a tactic which renders his enduring legacy to football a dubious one. Several contemporaries nominate him as the innovator of the notorious 'offside trap', a defensive ruse more generally ascribed to Bill McCracken of Newcastle United (1904–23). In Bert Morley's sole England appearance – 1–1 against Ireland in Belfast in 1910 – the much-reviled tactic proved largely ineffective.

MORRELL, LADY OTTOLINE VIOLET ANNE, English aristocrat, society hostess, fulsome patron of the Bloomsbury Group, and self-professed devotee of Burnley Football Club, died at Tunbridge Wells, Kent, on April 21, 1938.

Born in London on June 16, 1873, Lady Morrell is the earliest female incarnation of the 'celebrity fan' and a pioneering example of the breed of 'literati turned soccerati' later to become ubiquitous. Although resident in the south, it was through her marriage in 1902 to would-be Liberal politician Philip Edward Morrell that her declared infatuation for the Lancashire side ensued. He was MP for Burnley 1910–18, during which time his incurably romantic wife made studious visits to Turf Moor, the home ground of Burnley FC, in order to 'commune with the people'.

Her support reached fever pitch when Burnley beat Liverpool 1–0 in the 1914 FA Cup Final at the Crystal Palace, after which she hosted with her husband a victory reception for the team and officials at which she drank freely from the Cup and embraced her Burnley heroes with no little enthusiasm. She later wrote girlishly in a letter to the philosopher Bertrand Russell that 'they look upon me as their mascot'.

She had an 'open marriage', conducting overt affairs with both men and women, among the latter the artist Dora Carrington. Lady Morrell's many male friends included the author D.H. Lawrence and some critics consider her to be the inspiration for his Lady Chatterley. Lady Morrell was 64 at her death and was survived by her daughter Julian and by her one-time hero Bert Freeman, scorer of Burnley's only Cup-winning goal, who died in August 1955, aged 70.

MORTEN, ALEXANDER, an amateur goalkeeper for Wanderers (1865–74), died in New York on September 16, 1916. Although his birth date has been the subject of debate, the consensus is that he was born in Middlesex in 1831. If so he died aged 85 and enjoyed a mid-life experience which his countrymen of a future age would harbour only as a fantasy.

On March 8, 1873 – when thought to be 41 years and 114 days old – he made his England debut, captaining his country to a 4–2 triumph over Scotland. He never played again, but remains the oldest England debutant of all time, although yet to be officially recognised by the FA. The *Football Annual* said of him: 'His motto between the posts is *toujours prêt* – he is both fine in temperament and withstands the severest pressure with equanimity.' No man born earlier has ever played for England, and he was the first goalkeeper to captain any international side.

MULCASTER, RICHARD, headmaster, educational visionary, humanist and poet, who died at Stamford Rivers, Essex, on April 15, 1611, and was born in Carlisle, Cumbria, in 1531, has been expressly noted for his far-sighted advocacy of the beneficial effects of football at a time when much of Elizabethan England despised the pastime's very being.

Born into the gentry, Mulcaster was educated at Eton, Cambridge and Oxford. In 1561 he became the first headmaster of Merchant Taylor's School in London, at that time the largest in the country. In his publication of 1581 – *Positions Wherein those Primitive Circumstances Be Examined Which Are Necessary for the Training Up of Children* – he espoused the cause of small-sided *football* as an antidote to the reviled 'mob game' and was the first to refer to teams ('sides'), positions ('standings'), the benefits of a referee ('judge over the parties') and a coach ('trayning maister'). Let his own words be his testimonial:

> Consider the footeball play, which could not possibly have growne to this greatness that it is now if it had not had great helpes both to health and strength. Some small number sorted into standings, not meeting with their bodies so boisterously, nor shouldering so barbarously, may use footeball for much good. It strengtheneth and brawneth the whole body, it helpeth weak hammes, and by provoking superfluities downeward, it dischargeth the head and upper partes, drives downe the stone and gravel from both bladder and kidneies, and is good for the bowells.

Mulcaster was a man ahead of his time, for his pedagogical theories on the way football should be played were not generally accepted until at least 250 years after his death, thereafter earning him a lofty sobriquet bestowed by the game's antiquarians, 'The Father of Modern Football'.

NABOKOV, VLADIMIR VLADIMIROVICH, the Russian-American writer, best known for his novel *Lolita* (1955), died on July 2, 1977, in Switzerland, at the Montreux Palace Hotel, where he had lived for the past 17 years. Born in St Petersburg, Russia, on April 22, 1899, he displayed in adulthood a conspicuous urge to promote the cause of goalkeeping, missing no opportunity to elucidate his own peculiar grasp of the custodial art, which he honed in England.

After his family left Russia as exiles, he studied at Trinity College, Cambridge, for whom he kept goal in distinctive style. In his autobiography *Speak Memory* (1967) he wrote: 'Of the games I played at Cambridge, soccer has remained a windswept clearing in the middle of a rather muddled period. I was crazy about goalkeeping.'

The passage proceeds – 'Aloof, solitary, impassive . . . the keeper is the lone eagle, the man of mystery . . . he vies with the matador and the flying ace as an object of thrilled adulation' – and then concludes: 'I was less the keeper of a goal than the keeper of a secret. As with folded arms I leant my back against the left post, I enjoyed the luxury of closing my eyes, and thus I would listen to my heart knocking and feel the blind drizzle on my face and hear, in the distance, the broken sounds of the game, and think of myself as a fabulous exotic being in an English footballer's disguise, composing verse in a tongue nobody understood about a remote country nobody knew. Small wonder I was not very popular with my teammates.'

Nabokov never played professionally. In an interview for American television in 1965 he ruminated: 'I was erratic but rather spectacular. My last game was in Berlin in 1936. I was knocked out.' Consistent with the goalkeeping fraternity's reputation for eccentricity, Nabokov was a passionate lepidopterist known for his 'joyful promiscuity' in catching butterflies, but also becoming a distinguished expert in the classification of species through microscopic examination of their reproductive organs. His personal 'genitalia cabinet' housed abundant samples. He was also troubled, or some say blessed, by synaesthesia, a complex condition in which the 'sufferer' associates certain letters or numbers with particular colours, and was a composer of chess problems. Nabokov was 78 when he died, having never learned to drive a car.

NAIRN, SUSAN, whose funeral took place at St Mary's Parish Church, Hale, on Monday May 9, 1999, suffered one of the cruellest misfortunes in football-related history. Recently divorced and in straitened circumstances, she lived alone in Ditchfield Place, Ditton, Cheshire, and had landed a Littlewoods Pools jackpot of £561,020, but collapsed at home only hours before she was due to collect the cheque. Mrs Nairn had suffered a brain haemorrhage and died a few days later in the neuro-surgery department of Walton Hospital, Liverpool.

She had completed her coupon for many years with only modest success and was also a keen bingo player. At the Gala bingo hall in Widnes a member of staff said: 'Susan was very popular. We will miss her terribly. She quite often had good luck.' Mrs Nairn was aged 46 when the tragedy occurred.

NELSON, VICE-ADMIRAL HORATIO, 1ST VISCOUNT, the British naval hero born on September 29, 1758 at Burnham Thorpe, Norfolk, died at the Battle of Trafalgar on October 21, 1805. He is the only notable historic figure to whom blame has been apportioned for a club's failure to win promotion. In 1995–96 Blackpool FC were denied automatic advancement to Division One on the final day of the season, and in the subsequent play-off semi-finals they squandered a 2–0 lead established at Bradford City by losing 3–0 in the Bloomfield Road return. Manager Sam Allardyce was summarily sacked and a number of the club's more superstitious supporters advanced the theory that 'the curse of Lord Nelson' continued to blight Blackpool's progress. It was said this was because the club's boardroom had once been panelled with oak timbers shamelessly plundered from one of Nelson's stricken flagships.

The vessel was the *Foudroyant* – launched in Plymouth in 1798 – which when touring the British coast as an historic 'exhibition ship' ran ashore at Blackpool in severe gales on the morning of Wednesday June 16, 1897, two years before Bloomfield Road became the football club's headquarters.

The former Football League club Nelson FC boasts a more propitious link with the naval hero, being representatives of the Lancashire mill town named in his honour. Known as the Admirals, their great claim to fame is in beating Real Madrid 4–2 in a summer tour match in May 1923, the first British club to defeat the Spanish giants on their own ground.

Lord Nelson's parting words at his death have oft been disputed, but are said to have been 'Thank God I have done my duty.' Blackpool's sacked manager was slow to comprehend their possible resonance in connection with his own cruel fate. When interviewed by the BBC in May 2001 Sam Allardyce bemoaned: 'To this day I cannot understand why Blackpool sacked me.'

NEVILL, CAPT. WILFRED PERCY 'BILLIE', born in London on July 14, 1894, died aged 21 on Saturday July 1, 1916, the first day of the Battle of the Somme. A graduate of Jesus College, Cambridge, where he excelled at sport, Billie Nevill is one of the best-known soldiers of the Great War, as a result of his novel idea to lead his men forward across no-man's-land kicking footballs ahead of them.

Nevill initiated the advance with a hefty kick, after offering a prize to the first man to goal the leather in enemy trenches. Ground was taken, but he was unable to present the reward, for he was shot dead just short of the German lines.

The regiment – The Eighth Battalion East Surreys – suffered grave losses, but on account of Nevill's initiative they assumed heroic status. In Britain the unusual action stood for courage and strength of character. In Germany it was seen as a clear example of British madness, an early incarnation of the 'Barmy Army'.

Nevill was described in the press as 'both reckless and impossibly brave'. Two of the iconic footballs survived him – now held in English museums – and the episode was celebrated in verse. He is buried at Carnoy Military Cemetery.

On through the hail of slaughter,
Where gallant comrades fall,
Where blood is poured like water,
They drive the trickling ball.
The fear of death before them,
Is but an empty name,
True to the land that bore them,
The Surreys play the game!

'Touchstone', 1916

NOVELLI, PHILIP CHARLES, outside-left for Old Etonians, whose FA Cup winner's medal was gained in a stiff breeze at the Kennington Oval on March 25, 1882 at the expense of Blackburn Rovers – a victory which represented the last glorious page in the history of the southern amateur in that competition – died at 11 Idol Lane, City of London, on December 4, 1905, leaving £4,240.

At Trinity College, Cambridge, he failed to attain his soccer blue, but became an accomplished player described by *The Sportsman* as 'a good side, works hard on and sticks to the ball'.

Born in Marylebone on September 17, 1857, his Italian merchant antecedents had emigrated from Piedmont, and at the time of his death, aged 48, his home was at Morden Holt, Datchet, Buckinghamshire. He was an ardent oarsman – in 1876 he stroked the Eton eight – and gained a widespread reputation as a merchant banker.

OTTAWAY, CUTHBERT JOHN, to whom fell the honour in 1872 of being the first captain of an England association football team, died whilst still in the full vigour of his powers at 34 Westbourne Place, Eaton Square, London, on April 2, 1878, his entire estate amounting to barely £800.

He was a centre-forward – 'fast and very skilful, his beautiful science exhibiting how a ball ought to be taken through a host of foes'. His singular honour was bestowed in the world's first official international – England's 0–0 draw with Scotland at the West of Scotland Cricket Ground, Partick, near Glasgow, on November 30, 1872. In his only other England appearance – again as captain in 1874 – Scotland emerged 2–1 victors at the same venue.

Ottaway also captained Oxford University to their 1874 FA Cup Final win and twice finished runner-up, once with Old Etonians. He played besides for Marlow and Crystal Palace. An exemplar of the multi-talented amateur sportsman, at Brasenose College, Oxford (1870–73) he won blues in soccer, athletics, rackets, real tennis and cricket. At the latter he played twice for Kent, seven times for Middlesex, and in three seasons for the Gentlemen v. the Players, then cricket's most significant honour. In his first-class career (1869–76) he scored 1,691 runs at an average 27.27 and as wicketkeeper bagged 22 catches and one stumping.

He withdrew from mainstream sport in 1876 to become a barrister, having left Oxford with a First in Moderations and a Third in Classics. Born at Dover, Kent, on July 20, 1850, he had attained only 27 years and 250 days when time was called, his Canadian-born wife Maria surviving him and his daughter Lillian being born after his death. The demise of England's first captain was the result of complications arising from a chill, said by some to have been caught 'in the course of a night's dancing'.

OWEN, ELIAS, goalkeeper for Wales in the three Home International matches of 1884, and brother of the Welsh international winger William Pierce Owen, died at Ruthin, Denbighshire, on September 20, 1888, aged only 25. Born in 1863 at Llanllechid, Caernarvonshire, his father was the Reverend Elias Owen, the authority on Welsh folklore whose unshakeable belief in dragons and fairies was vividly documented in his works.

Elias junior played his club football with Ruthin (1880–85), starting as a half-back and converting to goalkeeper in 1882. His performances against Ireland and England drew the comment from the selectors that Owen had 'acquitted himself well, and it will be a difficult matter to entrust the important task of defending goal to a more competent player'. In the next game against Scotland he let in four goals and was dropped for good.

The manner of his death four years later might be considered untypical of later breeds of international goalkeeper. At the end of three years' assiduous study of theology at Lampeter College he took his own life while depressed over the outcome of his final examinations.

PAGE, LOUIS ANTONIO, born in Kirkdale, Liverpool, on March 27, 1899, died aged 60 on October 12, 1959. A flying left-winger, equally potent at centre-forward, he played seven times for England (1927–28). He achieved a unique double international standing, for he also represented England at baseball, as did his three brothers – John, Bill, and Tommy – who were also professional footballers. His League career comprised 421 League games (1919–32) – the majority for Northampton Town and Burnley – and 138 goals. In Burnley's 7–1 away win at Birmingham City in April 1926, Page bagged three goals in each half – the only Burnley player ever to score a double hat-trick. He later managed Yeovil, Newport County, Swindon Town and Chester, but without conspicuous success. He had cheated death during the First World War – while serving in the Royal Navy his vessel HMS *Virginian* was torpedoed – but was unable to survive the painful illness which ended his life in hospital at Birkenhead. In 1991 his daughter Phil chronicled the unusual dynasty in *Liverpool's Sporting Pages*.

PARR, LILIAN, who died on May 24, 1978, aged 72, and was laid to rest in her native St Helen's, was once considered 'the finest lady footballer in the world'. Born on April 26, 1905, the working-class winger made her name with the celebrated Dick, Kerr Ladies, who in the twenties played to huge crowds for charity, the 53,000 at Goodison Park on Boxing Day 1920 being their record.

In her debut season aged only 14 she scored 43 goals, and by the time she retired aged 46 in 1951 had notched close to 1,000 successful strikes. A team-mate said of her: 'Lily Parr was a one-off. Close to six feet tall, with jet-black hair, rather uncouth and ungainly, but with great skill and a tremendously powerful shot. She was extremely shy but a joker, and a loveable rogue. Shall we say she "removed things" – signed match balls especially, which she sold to keep her in Woodbine cigarettes.'

After leaving the employ of the Dick, Kerr engineering company, Lily Parr became a nurse, and a few years into retirement bravely endured a double mastectomy, saying: 'It's taken me 62 years to grow these buggers, now they've taken them off me.' When cancer finally claimed her ten years later she left no husband or family – Lily had remained unmarried, living for many years with her partner Mary in Preston.

In 2002 – in the company of Sir Bobby Charlton, Sir Stanley Matthews and Eric Cantona – Lily Parr became an inaugural inductee in the National Football Museum's 'Hall of Fame', the first female so honoured.

PATERSON, JAMES EDMUND 'NEIL', Academy Award-winning screenwriter and novelist, and much-respected former skipper of Dundee United, died aged 79 in Crieff, Scotland, on April 19, 1995, his informal epitaph – 'the most literary footballer of all time' – unlikely to be superseded.

Born in Greenock, Scotland, on December 31, 1915, and brought up in Banff, where his father practised law, it was at Edinburgh University that the author known as Neil Paterson cultivated a twin passion for the more usually disparate bedfellows 'writing' and 'football'. Playing first for Buckie Thistle and Leith Athletic, he signed for the Scottish League Division Two side Dundee United on July 1, 1936, the erudite newcomer being swiftly elected captain by his team-mates, an admirably non-judgemental gesture considering he was by then writing boy-meets-girl short stories for women's magazines.

Despite conspicuous talent as a forward Paterson remained an amateur and left United at the end of the 1936–37 season to write.

He married Rose MacKenzie in 1939 and after war service spent mainly on minesweepers penned his debut novel *On My Faithless Arm* (1946) under the pseudonym John Kovack, winning an Atlantic Award for Literature. Further novels and countless short stories followed, but screenplays were Paterson's preferred genre – in 1959 he adapted John Braine's novel *Room at the Top* for cinema, the acclaimed result earning him the Hollywood Oscar more usually bestowed upon footballers only metaphorically. Of almost a dozen films on which Paterson worked as writer, two attained minor cult status – *The Kidnappers* (1953) and *Innocent Sinners* (1958).

He retired from regular authorship in his forties, moving to Perthshire where he pursued golf and salmon fishing and took up key appointments in the arts – he became a board member of Grampian Television (1960–86) and The Arts Council for Great Britain (1974–76), also governor of the British Film Institute (1958–60).

Neil Paterson remains the only footballer fulsomely praised by both Somerset Maugham – 'a wonderfully amusing book, I only wish it had been longer' – and H.E. Bates – 'disarming simplicity, a triumph by means of artless detail' – and one reviewer called him 'the best Scottish-born story-teller since Robert Louis Stevenson'. Paterson appeared in 26 Scottish League games for Dundee United, scoring nine goals, and as a writer he was critically acclaimed on both sides of the Atlantic. A number of his works were translated into both Swedish and Braille.

PAYNE, JOSEPH, who from 1934 to 1947 scored a remarkable 109 goals in 118 League games, died aged 61 in April 1975. Born in 1914 in the mining village of Brimington Common, near Chesterfield, he signed for Luton Town after being spotted playing for Bolsover Colliery. On Easter Monday 1936 he scored ten goals in Luton's 12–0 win over Bristol Rovers – remarkably his first outing at centre-forward, promoted from wing-half in an injury crisis. The astonishing feat established a League record unlikely to be beaten. His form continued with 55 League goals for Luton the next season, but later spells with Chelsea and West Ham United proved less productive.

Joe Payne was selected only once for England (1937), scoring two goals, and in the same year played Minor Counties cricket for Bedfordshire. During the war he twice broke an ankle, and retired from the first-class game in 1947 dogged by ill health. The former coal-miner was 22 years old at the time of his sensational baptism as a striker – he was known thereafter as 'Ten Goal Payne'.

PEMBER, ARTHUR, who has been called the 'mystery man' of early football, was born in New Park Road, Brixton, London, in 1835. As the first president (1863–67) of the Football Association, he played a central role in shaping the game's Laws. Yet, after he died aged 50 in La Moure, Dakota, United States, on April 3, 1886, his *New York Times* obituary was unmatched in his homeland.

Unusually for a soccer pioneer, he attended neither public school nor university, being educated at home by aunts. He entered his father's profession of stockbroker, and was founder and captain of the Kilburn No Names football club, composed largely of City financiers. While at the FA, he presided over the banning of 'handling' and 'hacking', thereby cementing the seminal distinction between 'association football' and 'rugby football' which conceived the game.

His remarkable life bears scrutiny. In 1860 he married Elizabeth Hoghton, who died nine months later following a miscarriage. In 1862 he wed 17-year-old Alice Mary Grieve, who bore him ten children, although several died in infancy. During his FA tenure, Pember incubated radical personal ideas. He joined the religious movement of Ritualism, and predicted both the demise of the House of Lords and that Britain would become a republic.

Such views not only alienated his peers but hastened his emigration in 1868 to New York, where he became a freelance journalist specialising in 'undercover assignments'.

As 'Amateur Vagabond' he donned convincing disguises to live the 'low life', becoming in turn a miner, circus hand, beggar, engine driver, bargeman, hawker and prisoner. The stories were published to acclaim in *Mysteries and Miseries of New York* (1874). Some literary sleuths believe the creator of Sherlock Holmes, Sir Arthur Conan Doyle (q.v.), read the book and based the detective's penchant for disguise on the persona of the former FA president. It is also claimed that Doyle's story *The Man with the Twisted Lip* – about a respectable gent disguised as a beggar – was a thinly veiled rewrite of one of Pember's yarns.

After his second wife died of typhoid in 1881, Pember travelled west to start a new life as a farmer in La Moure, North Dakota, but soon perished there from kidney failure. No football 'high-hat' has been more colourful or so stealthily marginalised by his peers. His handlebar moustache spanned eight inches, and he is thought to be the only FA president to have fully ascended Mont Blanc.

PRIESTLEY, JOHN BOYNTON, the English writer and broadcaster, born in Bradford, Yorkshire, on September 13, 1894, died on August 14, 1984. In his novel *The Good Companions* (1929), he rationalised working-class spectatorship in terms frequently since invoked: 'To say that these men paid their shillings to watch 22 hirelings kick a ball is merely to say that a violin is wood and catgut, that *Hamlet* is so much paper and ink. For a shilling the Bruddersford United AFC offered you conflict and art.'

His further observation – 'Through a turnstile into another and altogether more splendid kind of life, hurtling with conflict and yet passionate and beautiful in its art' – may be regarded as the progenitor of the latter-day sobriquet 'the beautiful game', usually attributed to Pelé.

Priestley was once an ardent practitioner: 'In my boyhood and youth I played a good deal of soccer, always at full-back, and could play hard against some very tough opponents.' He was an admirer of Bradford City, although hard to please, and in later life his interest waned. In a letter to John Arlott (q.v.) in 1972 he wrote: 'I never see soccer now, except on television. There's too much tension, too much money and publicity. I never enjoyed our side that rather luckily collected the World Cup. Somehow Ramsey took the panache and sparkle out of the game.'

J.B. Priestley died aged 89 in his native Yorkshire.

RACE, PENNY, the first 'footballer's wife' of the modern age to receive
wide media exposure, died in a car crash in Monza, Italy, in 1995.
The circumstances of the accident remain shrouded in mystery, as
does Penny's true age, although the dates on her tombstone suggest
she was 41 when tragedy struck.

She was born Penny Laine and became secretary to Ben
Galloway, the well-known manager of Melchester Rovers. On St
Valentine's Day 1976 she proposed to the Rovers and England
centre-forward Roy Race, and they were married in May that
year – with a reception in the Melchester supporters' club. On
May 21, 1977, Penny gave birth to twins – Roy Chester, better
known as 'Rocky', and Melinda Penny – and a second daughter,
Diana, was born on July 10, 1982, the result of an emotional rec-
onciliation after Penny and Roy had briefly split the year before.

Tragedy first visited the family in 1993 when Roy lost his left
foot in a helicopter accident. He recovered to become manager
of AC Monza in Italy, where his beloved 'Pen' suffered her fatal
crash. She was much admired by generations of young boys, some
of whom in maturity have not been ashamed to admit that her
neatly drawn curves were the means by which their ardour was
first fully raised by a member of the female sex.

READITT, SGT. JOHN, VC, who with his father had been supplier and
repairer of football boots to Manchester United FC, died after a
protracted illness on June 9, 1964, aged 67. The family, whose clog
shop was on Ashton New Road, Clayton, were awarded the pres-
tigious ten-year footwear contract shortly before the First World
War began in August 1914. Seventeen-year-old John, born in

Manchester on January 19, 1897, became a private in the Sixth Battalion South Lancashire Regiment, earning his Victoria Cross on February 25, 1917, attacking a Turkish stronghold in Mesopotamia.

At Alqayat-al-Gaharbigah Bend, the fearless 20-year-old advanced five times along a water course in the face of heavy machine-gun fire, being the sole survivor on each occasion. After his officer had been killed he made several more brave forays against the 1,500-strong enemy on his own initiative, holding key strategic ground until support arrived.

He later achieved the rank of sergeant and was discharged in July 1919, whereupon he returned to fulfil the remainder of the boot contract. A keen amateur footballer, he was survived by his wife Lily, whom he had married in 1921. They are buried together in Gorton Cemetery, Manchester. On April 27, 2000, John Readitt's medal was auctioned by Spink of London – it sold for eight times its estimate, to a private buyer for £40,000.

RENNY-TAILYOUR, COL. HENRY WAUGH, managing director of the Arthur Guinness and Co. Brewery, Dublin, and scorer in 1873 of Scotland's first international goal, died at his home near Montrose, Forfarshire, on June 15, 1920, and is buried in the town's Rosehill Cemetery. Of his pioneering days as an amateur centre-forward a team-mate said of him: 'Renny had the happy knack of scoring goals when they were most needed.' His one full Scottish cap (1873) was matched by a rugby appearance for his country against England (1872), making him the only player to have represented Scotland in both football codes.

Born at Mussoorie, North-West Province, India, on October 9, 1849 – while his Scottish father was serving in the army there – he grew up on the family estate at Newmanswalls, close to Montrose, attending Cheltenham College before entering the British Army. He played in three FA Cup Finals for the Royal Engineers, his contribution to the Sappers' sole victory (1875) being crucial – in the drawn first game (1–1) against Old Etonians he scored the equaliser – according to *The Sporting Life* 'it glanced off Renny-Tailyour's knee through the posts' – and was credited with both goals in the 2–0 replay victory.

A friend remarked that 'he was a better cricketer than footballer' – playing three times for the Gentlemen against the Players, the highest accolade available in pre-Test days. He also turned out for Kent (1873–83) and the Engineers (1870–88) – scoring 12,291 runs for the regimental side at an average of 44, including 52 centuries and a 331 not out against the Civil Service.

No finer all-rounder ever joined the Engineers' ranks – at the Royal Military Academy sports in 1870 he won the mile and half-mile races, and against Sandhurst defeated all comers at throwing the cricket ball. In later years he took to fishing, shooting and golf. His association with the Guinness Company began in 1899 at the close of his distinguished military career, and he had retired from his post barely a year when his death occurred, aged 70. Latterly he has received the rare epithet 'a Montrose great', enthusiasts of the Gable Endies having divined that in 1887–88 he was appointed honorary president of the club.

RIPPER, JACK (THE), a notorious killer to whom no firm identity or death date has ever been attached, may or may not have been a football devotee, but secures his place in the game's alternative annals via the fertile imagination of the fictional 1950s schoolboy Nigel Molesworth.

The anarchic pupil of St Custard's Prep School selected the murderer at centre-forward in his eclectic 'World XI' – Goliath, Romulus, Remus, Skool Dog, Self, Richard I, Julius Caesar, Cain, Jack the Ripper, Livy, and Esau – which remains one of the great fantasy sides in football history. Molesworth was the inspired creation of Geoffrey Willans and thought by his admirers 'the greatest

schoolboy ever to stalk the earth'. Through his wildly original spelling his winter game of choice was habitually transmogrified to 'foopball'.

Not content with literary allusion alone, some Ripperologists have sought to link the 'Whitechapel Murderer' to the game at large, noting the curiosity that no less than two men on the 'suspect' list were intimates of the England centre-forward Harry Chester Goodhart (q.v.). It has also been remarked upon that the Ripper's second victim Annie Chapman was killed on Saturday September 8, 1888 – the inaugural day of Football League matches – although this has yet to be proven significant.

ROBLEDO, EDUARDO 'TED' OLIVER, wing-half for Newcastle United in the 1950s, lost his life at sea, in mysterious circumstances, on December 6, 1970, aged 42. Born in Iquique, Chile, on July 26, 1928, he came to England with his family at the age of four. In his teens he joined Barnsley with his older brother Jorge 'George' and in January 1949 the inseparable pair moved to Newcastle United. Their appearance in the 1952 Cup Final victory over Arsenal marked the first time that two overseas players had been included in a Cup Final side. George scored the only goal.

After 37 League games for Newcastle, Ted returned to Chile to play for the famous Santiago club Colo Colo, but before retiring in 1957 made two final appearances in England for Notts County. He then worked at sea and while serving on the oil tanker the *Al Sahn* in the Persian Gulf went missing overboard and was assumed drowned. It was rumoured that he had been cast off the vessel by the ship's captain, who was charged with murder but acquitted on grounds of insufficient evidence – Ted Robledo's body was never found.

His brother George, considered the more talented player, was a wary traveller. He had an irrational fear of bus journeys and invariably went to away matches by train on his own. His career ended in Chile, where he died of a heart attack on April 1, 1989. The Robledo brothers were fondly remembered in England – one Barnsley supporter labelled them 'unmistakeable exotics in a drab grey world'.

ROWLEY, GEORGE 'ARTHUR', a revered inside-forward at both Leicester City and Shrewsbury Town, died on December 19, 2002, aged 76. He scored more League goals in his career than any other player in history – 434 in 619 games – achieved with West Bromwich Albion, Fulham, Leicester City and Shrewsbury between 1946 and 1965. A pen-picture said that he 'has a thunderbolt left peg and burly physique, with great aerial power and lethal on the ground'.

Arthur Rowley never won a full international cap – yet his less prolific brother Jack played six times for England while at Manchester United. After hanging up his boots Rowley had less happy spells as a manager – he fell out with Sheffield United and was sacked by Southend, where he was ironically labelled 'too defensive'. Born in Wolverhampton on April 21, 1926, his first club on leaving school was Wolverhampton Gas Works. A colleague said in his memory: 'Arthur's fame will enter the record books, but what will not be recorded is his shy and reserved nature, which hid a football brain and a fierce determination bent on total success for both him and the team.'

ROWLEY, WILLIAM SPENCER, a centre-forward turned goalkeeper twice capped by England (1889–92), died in 1939 in America, where he had emigrated. Born in Hanley, Stoke-on-Trent, in 1865, he began with Port Vale but changed allegiance to Stoke City in 1886. Described by journalist Jimmy Catton (q.v.) as 'always judicious, splendidly cool, and one of the cleverest men who ever stood between the posts', his performance at Preston North End in the opening game of 1889–90 belied the observation – Stoke were

beaten 10–0 as Rowley became the first goalkeeper to concede double figures in a Football League game.

Another record secured on March 5, 1892 was more welcome – playing for England against Ireland in Belfast he became the first goalkeeper to save a penalty kick in an international game, when Samuel Torrance failed to convert. Billy Rowley played 118 League games for Stoke over eight seasons, refusing to allow a broken breastbone sustained in 1890–91 to hamper his progress.

Between 1896 and 1898 he served as the club's secretary-cum-manager, a tenure fraught with difficulty. On several occasions he was obliged to pay transfer fees from his own pocket, and in August 1898 was suspended by the League after transferring himself to Leicester Fosse and agreeing his own signing-on fee. Shortly before that indignity three of his Stoke players had been suspended by the club for drinking champagne during pre-season training. Rowley was permitted to play only once for Fosse prior to returning to Stoke. He became a postman and well-known publican before retiring to anonymity in the United States.

SABINE, HENRY WILMSHURST, a long-serving branch manager with the London, City and Midland Bank, who at various times in the late Victorian era captained the football, cricket and hockey clubs in his native Oswestry, Shropshire, died in Harrogate, Yorkshire, on August 13, 1955, at the age of 90. He was born on January 9, 1865, the son of a solicitor, and 'on grounds of partial ancestry' played once for Wales at outside-right, in 1887, when he recorded their only goal in a shock 4–1 reversal against Ireland in Belfast.

That he attained such an advanced age suggests that Sabine was dealt a propitious hand in the game of life, but arguably the fates were fickle. He was awarded a Royal Humane Society medal in 1892 for saving the life of a person about to drown in the River Severn, but his own life was lost cheaply. The cause of death was one oft alluded to but rarely an actuality – on his way to the county ground in Harrogate to watch a cricket match the sprightly nonagenarian was run over by a bus.

SARTRE, JEAN-PAUL CHARLES AYMARD, political activist, novelist, playwright, and existentialist philosopher, died aged 74 on April 15, 1980, in Paris, where he was born in 1905. Considered a brilliant brain able to interpret the world's workings with astute clarity, his legacy to football was a pithy one: 'In football everything is complicated by the presence of the opposing team.' Such rhetoric so compelled his countrymen that over 20,000 Parisians attended his funeral procession.

SATINOFF, WILLIAM, a Manchester raincoat manufacturer, labelled 'the forgotten man of Munich', died aged 49 on February 6, 1958.

A close friend of the Manchester United manager Matt Busby, he was the only supporter allowed to travel with the club's official party to that year's European Cup tie against Red Star Belgrade in Yugoslavia. He was killed when the aircraft on the return journey crashed at Munich Riem airport the day following the game, while attempting take-off on a snowy runway after a routine refuelling stop.

His demise changed the course of United's history, for Satinoff had been expected to join their board and was hotly tipped as a future chairman. In his stead, only a day after the 'Munich Disaster', the Salford wholesale butcher Louis Edwards – later dubbed 'Champagne Louis' – was appointed a director. In 1965 he became chairman and with his son Martin ushered the club towards its present corporate persona.

Willie Satinoff is buried in the Jewish section of Manchester Southern Cemetery only yards from a busy pavement. Countless pedestrians passing his grave daily remain entirely ignorant of the tragic fate of its occupant. His company was 'Alligator Rainwear'.

SCATTERGOOD, ERNALD OAK, the 5ft 8in goalkeeper known as 'Ernie', who between 1907 and 1924 played 450 League games for Derby County and Bradford Park Avenue, died at Worksop, Nottinghamshire, on July 2, 1932. A florid name apart, his chief notability is as the top-scoring goalkeeper in Football League history, his eight strikes all coming from the penalty spot.

An ever-present in the Derby County team that won the 1911–12 Second Division title, he became the club's regular penalty-taker a season later. After scoring three out of three – according to a witness 'more by virtue of a powerful shot than any astute placing' – he joined Bradford in 1914. He survived being gassed in World War One before going on to complete 268 League games for them. Five further penalty kicks were routinely dispatched before an unusual incident persuaded him to stand down.

On Easter Saturday 1922 the South Shields goalkeeper Willis Walker saved one, and Scattergood was involved in a frantic race to return to his own line – cowed by the experience, he agreed to remain permanently 'at home' thereafter. In his sole appearance for England (1913) he let in three against Wales at Ashton Gate, but finished on the winning side in a seven-goal thriller.

Ernie Scattergood was born in the Derbyshire coal-mining village of Riddings on May 29, 1887, and was aged 45 at his death. His goalkeeping gene survived him but the penalty-taking instinct was eradicated – from 1933 to 1937 his son Kenneth played 65 League games in goal without once deserting his post.

SCOTT, SIR JAMES 'GEORGE', a diminutive Scottish journalist and colonial administrator, an intrepid and fearless explorer, and a keen footballer, died aged 83 on April 4, 1935. Born in Dairsie, Fife, on Christmas Day 1851, the son of a Scottish minister, he helped establish British colonial rule in Burma in the late nineteenth century. While there he introduced football to the country, employing the game's ethos 'to instil the British virtues of discipline and respect into a wild people'.

When not hacking his way through dense vegetation he was a teacher, and it was at St John's College, Rangoon that he kicked the first football on Burmese soil in 1878. On his extensive travels there he organised many Anglo-Burmese encounters in which he played himself, and was successful in inveigling warring hill-tribes to take each other on, noting in a memoir that 'the Burmese love the game, because it's just like fighting.'

He had a fondness for gargantuan pith helmets, and a bluffness of expression which bordered on caricature. No situation fazed him – an entry in his diary read: 'Stepped on something soft and wobbly. Struck a match and found it was a dead Chinaman. Had a sandwich and moved on.'

Of his many books on Burma – written as Shway Yoe – his most enduring is *The Burman – His Life and Notions* (1882), which records for posterity one of British football's lowliest hours: 'Before one Anglo-Burmese contest our goalkeeper Jerry Morrison was felled by a stomach bug, and his replacement, utterly baffled by the rules of the sport, only attempted to save shots that were going over the bar. The Burmese won 2–1.'

He was survived by his third wife – the author Geraldine Mitton – who wrote in her biography of him: 'My husband was a gifted linguist, who when confronted by the Wild Wa, a tribe of fierce head-hunters, won them over by telling a side-splitting joke.' Her account suggests too that 'George' Scott was well ahead of his time in matters sartorial, for he frequently adopted local dress, and as such was the first British footballer to wear a sarong.

SCOTT, SIR WALTER, the Scottish novelist, born in Edinburgh on August 15, 1771, died aged 61 on September 21, 1832 at his home Abbotsford, in the Borders. While never an accomplished player – he had a permanent limp from a bout of polio – he championed football's cause with conspicuous zeal, notably in the Borders, an area considered by some to be the very 'cradle of the game'.

His finest hour was at Carterhaugh, where on December 5, 1815, he orchestrated a celebrated 'big-side' match in which the men of Yarrow engaged the burghers of Selkirk, the ranks of the latter championed by Scott himself. His young son Walter was 'mascot' for the day – according to an Edinburgh newspaper 'he rode over the field displaying the banner amid the acclamations of the spectators' – which Scott afterwards professed to be his proudest moment as a father. In his poem for the occasion – *The Lifting of the Banner* – Scott observed that 'Life is itself but a game of football', anticipating its modern counterpart – 'Football is Life' – by almost two centuries.

SHOSTAKOVICH, DMITRI DMITRIEVICH, the foremost Russian composer of the Soviet era, born in St Petersburg on September 25, 1906, died in Moscow on August 9, 1975, aged 68. His twin passions were music and football. At the first he was a child prodigy – intense and obsessive – and carried the same traits into his relationship with the second. From his teens he maintained a ledger – his treasured 'Grossbuch' – in which he assiduously recorded statistics and trivia – reports, scores, transfers, line-ups, and curious League standings arranged in 'pyramids' of his own invention. More than a fan, he grew into a connoisseur. His son Maxim recalled, 'My father knew every footballer's name by heart.'

From the 1930s he became an ardent follower of Leningrad Zenit (now Zenit St Petersburg), cutting short his composing retreats in some rural idyll to return to the city for home games. Intellectual acquaintances found his behaviour surprising – the writer Maxim Gorky observed: 'He was a rabid fan, he comported himself like a little boy, leapt up, screamed, and gesticulated.' Shostakovich explained this knowingly: 'A football match is the only place where everyone can say out loud what he thinks and what he sees.'

He was one of the first composers to incorporate football into a musical work – his 1930 ballet *The Golden Age* – a satirical piece about a Soviet team visiting a western city, which included a referee's whistle in its score. He qualified as a referee – although never officiating seriously – and wrote a number of articles about football for the Soviet press. His interest in the game lasted into maturity – he planned to attend the 1966 World Cup in England, but was sorely disappointed when working commitments obliged him to cancel.

It has been said that his immersion in football reflected his innate obsessions. He washed his hands habitually, synchronised all his clocks to the second, and sent letters to himself to monitor the effectiveness of the postal service. He suffered ill health in later life, and broke two legs and one arm – even then his statistical bent led him to quip that he was '75 per cent to completing the full set'. He died from lung cancer, and was survived by his third wife, a son and a daughter. He left the game one pithy quote: 'Football is the ballet of the people.'

SOO, HONG Y 'FRANK', was an immensely popular wing-half and inside-forward. Either side of the Second World War he played 173 League games for Stoke City and 71 for Luton Town – the intervening conflict almost certainly denied him a full England cap. He died on January 25, 1991, knowing that he had been labelled 'the first "man of colour" to play for England, and the only footballer of Oriental extraction ever to do so.' His nine appearances for the national team were wartime and 'Victory' internationals classed as 'unofficial'.

Frank Soo was born in Buxton, Derbyshire, on March 8, 1914, his Chinese father Our Quong Soo having married English girl Beatrice Whittam six years earlier. Frank played for Liverpool Schoolboys and the Cheshire County League side Prescot Cables before signing for Stoke in January 1933. After his League career ended with Luton in 1947 he managed St Albans City before moving to Italy to take charge of Padova (1950–52). He had one season (1959–60) as boss of Scunthorpe United, but either side of that unhappy sojourn managed a host of Scandinavian clubs. His finest hour was in 1954–55, when he led the Stockholm club Djurgarden to their fifth Swedish Championship.

Cyril 'Sammy' Chung, who was born in Abingdon in 1932, the second of only two Britons of oriental extraction to play in the Football League, described Soo as 'a great inspiration'. The itinerant Frank Soo eventually returned to England and his death aged 76 was registered in Staffordshire. Sammy Chung, by then a well-known manager, survived him.

SOUTHWORTH, JOHN, the thrice-capped England centre-forward (1889–92) born in Blackburn on December 12, 1866, died on October 16, 1956, aged 89. The game's first truly prolific marksman, he was described in *Association Football and the Men Who Made It* (1906) as 'reasonably dreaded by every opponent in whatever class'. When only 16 he notched up six goals in one game for Blackburn Olympic and earned a special reputation for striking in Cup matches – with Blackburn Rovers in 1890 and 1891 he gained two FA Cup winner's medals. In his debut season with Everton he set the club record for scoring six in a match – against West Bromwich Albion in 1893–4 – and became the first player to reach 100 Football League goals. Throughout his career (1888–95) he amassed 133 goals in 139 games. Jack Southworth's skill was not confined to his feet – after retiring through injury in 1895 he became a professional violinist with Manchester's famous Hallé Orchestra.

SPENCER, HOWARD, an England captain and a legend at Aston Villa, died in Sutton Coldfield, aged 64, on January 14, 1940. Born in Edgbaston on August 23, 1875, he played 258 League games for Villa (1894–1907), won three FA Cup Finals, and was later a club director (1909–36). The 'Prince of Full-Backs' was said to be 'sporting, resourceful, and consummate in judgment'. Due to the vagaries of linguistic change – and the more liberal standards latterly attached to England captains – modern observers might mistakenly consider his talents to have been dubiously applied. A tribute penned after Spencer's passing said: 'After he finished playing he became a coke dealer, and died a very rich man.'

STANLEY, ARTHUR JOHN, late of Repton School and Trinity College, Cambridge, died on July 16, 1935, at 53 Lancaster Gate, London, within kicking distance of the Football Association headquarters. He was a regular inside-right for Clapham Rovers – described as 'a hard worker, generally on the ball' – with whom he gained an FA Cup winner's medal in 1880 when they beat Oxford University. He was a talented cricketer and a member of M.C.C., but a finer lawn tennis player. In both 1885 and 1886 he reached the final of the Wimbledon men's doubles in partnership with Claude Farrer, succumbing on each occasion to the near-unconquerable Renshaw twins.

By profession a member of the Stock Exchange, he was born in Paddington, London on June 26, 1853, and displayed in his will the not uncommon contemporary fear of being buried alive: 'I direct that before my burial my death shall be certified and confirmed by a qualified medical practitioner and that he shall also sever my jugular vein.' He was 82 when the final cut was made.

STATHAM, MAJ. FRANCIS 'LESLIE', MBE, known professionally as Arnold Steck, the military bandsman and composer, died aged 68 in April 1974, having earned an enduring place in football's popular culture. Born in Hatfield, on December 18, 1905, Leslie Statham was made Director of Music of the Welsh Guards in 1948, but retired from the army in 1962 to concentrate on composing. The genesis of his football celebrity can be traced precisely to 6.30 p.m. on BBC2 on August 22, 1964, when his 'Drum Majorette' introduced the first *Match of the Day* programme, a 3–2 home win for Liverpool over Arsenal. The rousing march became so embedded in the nation's psyche that it came to embody football itself. It remained the signature tune until 1971 when the current theme by Barry Stoller replaced it. The ultimate architect of Leslie Statham's unlikely celebrity survived him – the controller of BBC2 who first commissioned *Match of the Day*, Sir David Attenborough.

STUBBES, PHILIP, the Puritan pamphleteer and social commentator, had by his death *circa* 1610 left writings which render him the most vociferous calciophobe – a 'hater of football' – of all time.

His killjoy tendencies covered the full spectrum of Elizabethan pleasures – gluttony, sloth, gambling, play acting, promiscuity, excessive drinking and even maypole dancing – but the virulent attack reserved by Stubbes for football remains unmatched. His notorious work *The Anatomie of Abuses* (1583) stands as a lasting epitaph:

> For as concerning football playing I protest unto you it may rather be called a friendly kind of fight than a play or recreation, a bloody and murderous practise than a fellowly sport or pastime. For doth not everyone lie in wait for his adversary seeking to overthrow him and to pitch him on his nose so he can have him down. And he that can serve the most of this fashion, he is counted the only fellow and who but he? So that by this means sometimes their necks are broken, sometimes their backs, legs and arms, a part thrust out of joint, or their noses gush out blood and their eyes start out. And they have sleights to meet one betwixt two, to dash him against the heart with their elbows, to hit him under the short ribs with their gripped fists, and with their knees to catch him upon the hip and to pick him on his neck with a hundred such murdering devices. And hereof groweth envy, malice, rancour, hatred, displeasure, enmity and what not else, and sometimes fighting, brawling, contortion, quarrel-picking, murder, homicide and great effusion of blood, as experience daily teacheth. Is this murdering play now an exercise for the Sabbath day?

Stubbes was born *circa* 1555 and educated at both Oxford and Cambridge, but took no degree. For much of the time he travelled about the country, set apart from his fellow men by extreme moral fervour and godly zeal. He died in his fifties, survived by the evil pastime' he deplored, which in 1863 became the 'sanitised' game of association football now played routinely on Sundays to mass acclaim.

STUBBINS, ALBERT, the flame-haired Geordie 'goal ace' who became a hero on both Tyneside and Merseyside, died at his home in Cullercoats, on the north-east coast, on December 28, 2002. When Newcastle United met Liverpool at St James's Park a few days later, both sides wore black armbands in poignant memory of their former centre-forward.

Born in Wallsend, Tyne and Wear, on July 13, 1919 – but spending parts of his childhood in the United States – Stubbins first played for Newcastle United in 1937. Almost six feet tall, invariably labelled 'strapping', he scored a remarkable 237 goals in 218 matches during his time there, the prolific feat being sadly diminished since all but six of the strikes occurred in wartime 'friendlies'.

In his debut season at Liverpool his 24 goals made an immediate contribution to the team's 1946–47 League Championship triumph. In all games for the Reds he scored 83 times in 178 appearances, yet strangely was selected for England only once: an unofficial meeting with Wales in 1945, which England lost 1–0.

After Stubbins retired as a player (1953) he became a sports journalist, but briefly took charge of the semi-professional New York Americans at the beginning of the 1960s, the decade which spawned his most lasting and bizarre celebrity. This arose through his inclusion in the montage of 'famous people' featured on the cover of the iconic Beatles album *Sgt. Pepper's Lonely Hearts Club Band* (1967) – Stubbins was the only footballer so honoured, his grinning countenance appearing at the shoulder of movie legend Marlene Dietrich.

After his death aged 83 there were many words of tribute. Former England manager Sir Bobby Robson said, 'Stubbins was my childhood hero', but the most fitting epitaph – if not a little surreal – had already been supplied some years earlier in a telegram sent to the player by Paul McCartney: 'Well done Albert, for all those glorious years in football. Long may you bob and weave.'

STURGIS, JULIAN RUSSELL, a prominent novelist and playwright of his age, born in Boston, Massachusetts, United States, on October 21, 1848, died in London on April 13, 1904. On March 29, 1873 he became the first 'foreign-born' player to appear in an English Cup Final – the other 'overseas' finalists at that time had all been born in the British Empire to British parents – taking the laurel with Wanderers in their 2–0 defeat of Oxford University. The contest commenced in the morning so that the teams might later watch the Boat Race. *The Field* said of the game: 'With the deficit at 1–0 Oxford attempted the expedient of playing without a goal-keeper, a move which proved fatal to their hopes.' Sturgis was singled out as 'a most conspicuous forward' whose 'fine infusion of vigour' caught the casual eye.

At Eton he was Keeper of the Field (Captain of the football XI) and Chairman of Pop (the college debating society), and although a barrister by profession he earned his living as an author – Sturgis wrote the libretto for *Ivanhoe* (1891), the only grand opera by Sir Arthur Sullivan, for which he was much praised. He travelled widely in the Levant, where the natives little cared that he was the first American to play in an FA Cup Final, an honour generally attributed to John Harkes of Sheffield Wednesday, in 1993. Sturgis met his end at 16 Hans Road, Chelsea, aged 55, leaving the considerable sum of £79,435.

SUMMERS, JOHN HENRY, a journeyman forward born in Hammersmith, London, on September 10, 1927, died aged 34 in 1962. His 338 League games (1949–61) – for Fulham, Norwich, Millwall and Charlton Athletic – produced 174 goals. On December 21,

1957, during the Division Two game between Charlton and Huddersfield Town at The Valley, he engineered the most remarkable comeback in Football League history. Reduced to ten men from the 17th minute, Charlton trailed 2–0 at the interval and 5–1 with only 28 minutes remaining. Sporting a new pair of boots he had changed into at half-time – 'to break them in for the next game' – 'Johnny' Summers then scored five and made two as Charlton emerged 7–6 winners with the last kick of the match. Huddersfield are the only away side to score six goals in a League game and still lose. While their sorely chastened manager Bill Shankly learned well from the experience, the hero of the hour succumbed to cancer while still on Charlton's books.

T

TAYLOR, ALAN JOHN PERCIVALE, the eminent 'People's Historian' A.J.P. Taylor, died in a London nursing home on September 7, 1990, after a long battle with Parkinson's disease. Born in Birkdale, near Southport, Lancashire, on March 25, 1906, he demonstrated no obvious affection for football, but left for posterity an observation on England's seminal relationship with it – and the nation's diminishing place in world affairs – which in the fullness of time proved a shrewd one. Referring to the game's 1863 birth in London – when the British Empire was still a force to be reckoned with – Taylor wrote of the great English invention: 'By it the mark of England may well remain in this world when the rest of her influence has vanished.' The sage prophet was 84 at his death and had been three times married and twice divorced.

TAYLOR, JOHN DANIEL, the holder of a host of records at Everton, died on February 21, 1949, aged 77. Born in Dumbarton on January 27, 1872, his early promise with Dumbarton and St Mirren paved the way in 1896 for a big move south. He served Everton with rare distinction for 13 seasons, becoming the first player to make 400 appearances for the club and the only one in their history to play over 100 consecutive games. He was also the sole Everton man to participate in each of their FA Cup Finals of 1897, 1906 and 1907, in the second of which – the 1–0 defeat of Newcastle United – he became the first Everton captain to lift the trophy. His club record was 456 appearances and 80 goals.

Jack Taylor was a 'centre-half' – in those days an 'advanced play-maker' – but also a capable winger. He played four times for Scotland (1892–95) and suffered two cruel misfortunes. *The Jubilee*

History of the Everton Football Club relates how during the 1910 FA Cup semi-final he was 'struck a disabling blow to the larynx by a powerful shot'. Taylor never fully recovered from the unique injury, and spent his final days in non-League football. The second episode 39 years later precipitated his death, a misfortune again caused by a fast-moving projectile whose impact he failed to avert, on this occasion a motor car.

THAIN, JAMES, a retired airline pilot, died aged 54 on August 6, 1975, after falling ill at his poultry farm in Berkshire. The book *Captain Thain's Ordeal* (1973) dissects the pivotal moment in his life, which occurred on February 6, 1958, during what proved to be his final flight in command. Although in charge of the charter flight – British European Airways 609 Belgrade to Manchester – he had chosen to occupy the co-pilot's seat. Alongside him in the Airspeed Ambassador – G-ALZU *Lord Burghley* – was his close friend Captain Kenneth Rayment.

Following a scheduled refuelling stop at Munich the aeroplane crashed on its third attempt to take off in harrowing conditions, thick sludge preventing the craft reaching the necessary speed. There were 23 fatalities, among them eight members of the Manchester United team returning from a 'winning' 3–3 draw against Red Star Belgrade in the second leg of the European Cup quarter-final. The Munich air crash and the 'Busby Babes' who perished immediately entered the realms of football folklore.

Thain survived but never flew again. The West German authorities responsible for keeping the runway clear took legal action against him, harshly asserting that he had failed to clear ice from the plane's wings. He was dismissed by BEA on Christmas Day 1960 and only after 11 years of legal machinations was he finally cleared of any responsibility for the crash.

The ordeal perhaps took its toll, for his death resulted from a heart attack. Thain is buried in Warfield churchyard, Berkshire, and was survived by his wife Ruby Violet, who died November 27, 1998. Second-in-command Captain Rayment left the crash scene alive but died of his injuries nine days later.

TOWNLEY, WILLIAM, twice capped by England at outside-left, born in Blackburn on February 14, 1866, died on May 30, 1950. While playing for Blackburn Rovers he became the first man to score a hat-trick in an FA Cup Final, during the 6–1 victory over Sheffield Wednesday in 1890. He later assisted Darwen and Manchester City but achieved much greater fame on the Continent, where as a coach (1909–34) he was greatly instrumental in developing the game in Germany. Of the several clubs he managed there, particular success was achieved in 1920 with Bayern Munich. He also coached in Switzerland and guided the Dutch national team through the 1924 Paris Olympics. Billy Townley was one of the first English football coaches to make a significant impact abroad. His extended stint endured almost to his seventieth year, when he returned to England and eventually died there aged 84 in Blackpool.

TREVIS, ARTHUR STANLEY SACKVILLE REDVERS TREVOR BOSCAWEN GRIFFITH, a half-back known as 'Bos', sadly died aged 74 in 1984. Born in Blackheath, Worcestershire, in 1910, he began his football career with non-League Leamington Town and between 1936 and 1938 made 29 League appearances for Chester City after a solitary run-out with West Bromwich Albion.

In his veteran days he bolstered the ranks of Worcester City and died with his unique record still intact – the longest name in the history of League football – just edging out Blackpool's 1908 full-back Herbert Ernest Saxon Bertie Cordey Lyon, who with modest acquiescence was listed in programmes as Bert Lyon.

Trevis's proud claim was surpassed only when 'Charlie' Oatway (born in Hammersmith, November 28, 1973) made his League debut for Cardiff City in 1994–95. Oatway subsequently became a cult figure at Brighton and Hove Albion, where he played over 200 games. His pet forename was coined by his aunt, who suggested he would look 'a right Charlie' using the fuller version. His Queen's Park Rangers-obsessed parents had named their son in honour of the team's 1973 squad – Anthony Philip David Terry Frank Donald Stanley Gerry Gordon Stephen James Oatway.

TURNER, HELEN, known as 'The Bell', born in Yorkshire in 1920, but a well-known fan of Manchester City, died on Friday September 3, 2005, aged 85, having rung the praises of the club for over 30 years. Her peroxide blonde bun, generous frame and vigorously tolled bell first became familiar at Maine Road when City won the 1967–68 League Championship, and gained momentum when they won the 1969 FA Cup.

She ran a flower stall outside Manchester Royal Infirmary, and it became her habit each game to give a sprig of lucky heather to the City goalkeeper Joe Corrigan as he took occupancy between the posts. In order to maintain the ritual she once travelled all the way to Gretna Green to purloin the lucky charm, later ruminating that 'I'm not sure Joe always realises how much trouble I go to.'

When City won the 1976 League Cup she joined in the Wembley lap of honour, and at the club's last ever game at Maine Road in May 2003 enjoyed a standing ovation when at the age of 83 she responded noisily to the crowd's chanted command 'Helen, Helen, ring your bell.'

She was rather feared by the younger fans she kept in check on away trips, but was said to have had 'a heart of gold' and did a considerable amount for charity. She attended her final games in a wheelchair and following her death was honoured by a minute's silence at City's Eastlands Stadium. Helen 'The Bell' Turner was buried at Rochdale Cemetery, one of the last of that quaint but earthy breed of celebrity fan now seldom encountered.

VANN, LIEUT.-COL. THE REV. BERNARD WILLIAM, VC, was killed in action close to the village of Ramicourt, France, on October 3, 1918, aged 31. No more decorated footballer has appeared for a professional club, yet Vann fails to rank as 'a professional footballer awarded the Victoria Cross' since he played as an amateur for no remuneration. As such, Donald Bell VC (q.v.) of Bradford Park Avenue stands alone in the English professional ranks.

Bernard Vann was born at Rushden, Northamptonshire, on July 9, 1887. After graduating from Jesus College, Cambridge, he was ordained as a minister and became a schoolmaster. As a centre-forward he assisted Northampton Town and in 1906 played 12 games for Burton United (then a League club) before making three League appearances for Derby County in 1906–07 while teaching at Ashby Grammar School, Leicestershire. From 1913 until 1915 he was chaplain and history master at Wellingborough School, and in December 1917 he married Doris Victoria Beck, born in Ontario, Canada.

Instead of going to war as a padre, he cast off clerical dress, donned khaki, and went to the front with the Sherwood Foresters. His VC was won on September 29, 1918 at Bellenglise and Lehaucourt, France, when Lieutenant Colonel Vann led his battalion across the Canal du Nord through a thick fog and under heavy fire. When the advance was held up, he led the line forward to attack a battery of field guns, himself capturing three by shooting the artillerymen. The annals of the Sixth Battalion record that 'two German gunners were severely maimed by his riding crop'.

He was killed four days later by a sniper's bullet and was awarded his VC posthumously. During the course of the war he also won the Military Cross and Bar and, from the French, the Croix de Guerre with Palm Leaves. Chronology suggests that a productive liaison with his wife was effected a matter of weeks in advance of his heroic deeds, for their son Bernard Geoffrey Vann was born on June 2, 1919. The father he never saw is buried in France at Bellicourt British Cemetery.

VAUGHAN, JOHN OWEN, who in the 1880s won four caps at half-back for Wales when a leading player for his home town club Rhyl FC, died at Prestatyn, Flintshire, on October 5, 1952, at the commendable age of 89. Some might say his longevity was due reward for a watchful interest in the survival of others, for in his younger days Vaughan was a splendid swimmer said to have saved 'about a dozen people' from the sea at Rhyl. As such he is thought to be the only international footballer to have preserved a greater number of lives than he made appearances for his country.

Certain it is that in August 1886 he plucked a young woman from the water at his fourth attempt, and the following year saved a man and two children. For each of the rescues he was awarded a bronze medal by the Royal Humane Society. Sadly he was obliged to retire from football in 1888 when aged only 25, after undergoing several operations for eye trouble. He was born in Rhyl in 1863 and when he played in his school team at St Thomas's College they remained unbeaten for five years. Away from football he had worked in his father's bathing establishment and later as a draper's assistant. His death deprived the Prestatyn area of one of its leading authorities on coastal erosion.

VICTORIA, H.M. QUEEN, died aged 81 at Osborne House, on the Isle of Wight, on Tuesday, January 22, 1901, the longest-serving British monarch and the figurehead of a vast empire. Although mother to the first royal patron of the FA – the Prince of Wales in 1892 – Her Majesty paid scant heed to the pervasive virus of football euphoria which had characterised the latter part of her reign. Indeed her death in mid-season heralded an unprecedented disruption of the fixture list, the longest peacetime break in League football due to factors other than the weather.

As a mark of respect, all games scheduled for Saturday, January 26 were postponed, as were those for Saturday, February 2, the day of the funeral. A few Second Division games went ahead on February 9, but on account of FA Cup ties no First Division club played a League game until February 16, the unscheduled break for most clubs amounting to 28 days. Eight sides were obliged to wait until March for their next League game.

Victoria was born in London on May 24, 1819, becoming Queen in 1837, thereby presiding as monarch over the birth of association football and its progression into modernity. 'Victoria' was incorporated into the names of a number of clubs and playing enclosures in her honour. Her successor Edward VII, duly satisfied with the respect accorded his mother, agreed to continue as FA patron, thus establishing a royal tradition that continued thereafter.

VIDAL, REV. PREBENDARY ROBERT WALPOLE SEALY, England international and holder of a number of unassailable 'firsts' on the football field, died at Abbotsham Vicarage, Devon, on November 5, 1914. His early progress as a centre-forward was such that whilst still at Westminster School he was selected for England in the pre-official international against Scotland in 1870, aged 16 years 183 days. He was also the only player to gain an FA Cup winner's medal while still at school – for Wanderers in the first final (1872) – when, in laying on the only goal for M.P. Betts (q.v.), he became the first ever 'assistee' in a final tie.

By appearing in the 1873 FA Cup Final for Oxford University he became the first player to turn out for different clubs in two national Cup Finals, and in 1874 scored the opening and winning goal for Oxford in the inaugural Varsity match against Cambridge University. Vidal was good at many sports – he earned his rugby blue at Oxford (1873), played county cricket for Devon (1874), was a fine oarsman, and was founder and first president of the Oxford University Golf Club.

Ordained in 1877, he served as vicar of Abbotsham between 1881 and 1914, and in 1885 married Gertrude Molesworth, nine years his junior. He was born at Cornborough House, Abbotsham, near Bideford, on September 3, 1853, and when he died in the village aged 61 his funeral produced a huge turnout. He was the original 'Prince of Dribblers', a sobriquet later awarded often enough to others to become hackneyed.

WADE, GEORGE EDWARD, the celebrated British music hall comedian, better known by his stage name George Robey, died on November 29, 1954, at Saltdean, Sussex, aged 85. That his passing should occur during the season in which Chelsea were to finish League Champions, their first major honour, is tinged with poignancy, for Robey was a devotee of the club and in his Edwardian heyday had drawn on their lack of success for comedic effect, the first star to use football as such a vehicle. Indeed he began the long association between 'show business' and Chelsea, and was shamelessly indulged in 1907 when the club 'signed' him as an amateur after he had appeared and scored for them in a charity match. He was given a run out in the reserves and also played a number of games for the Millwall second string.

Robey may justly be labelled the first 'celebrity fan' and a pioneer of the charity match. In December 1905 he brought a team of professionals to Springfield Park, Wigan, to play against Wigan Town AFC in aid of the Chief Constable's Clog and Stocking Fund. In 1907 he raised £350 from a match which he organised and played in – Aston Villa 4 International XI 3. He was also the first to organise the breed of celebrity game by which 'showbiz' personalities were enabled to exercise their football vanities.

He became known as 'The Prime Minister of Mirth' and his most enduring 'football funny' proved reasonably prophetic: 'I have only joined Chelsea so as to keep them in the first League.' The son of a civil engineer, he was born at Herne Hill, London, on September 20, 1869, and received a knighthood in the year of his death.

WAINWRIGHT, ALFRED, MBE, the celebrated hill-walker, author and illustrator, who in 1939 co-founded the Blackburn Rovers Supporters Association, died of a heart attack on January 20, 1991, aged 84. Born in Blackburn on January 17, 1907, his guides to the Lake District achieved cult status, some selling to collectors for four-figure sums.

Wainwright's love of Rovers – to him unshakeably the best club in England – has been invoked to illustrate that peculiar nature of fandom whereby it is possible to find peace and solitude even in a crowd, for he craved in equal measure both the quiet of remote landscapes and the tumult of a packed Ewood Park.

His biographer Hunter Davies considered that both activities offered Wainwright an escape from reality, in particular his unhappy first marriage. His wife Ruth sometimes travelled to Blackburn matches on the same train as him but in a different carriage, and watched the game from a separate vantage point. She walked out on him in 1958.

Wainwright's sundry jottings on Rovers were read at a centenary celebration of his life held in Blackburn Cathedral in 2007. The chairman of the Wainwright Society said: 'The happiest I ever saw Alfred was one summery afternoon when we stood on a patch of grass with no real view to speak of – the centre circle at Ewood Park.'

WALDEN, FREDERICK INGRAM, an outside-right twice capped by England (1914 and 1922), died aged 61 in Northampton, on May 3, 1949. Born in Wellingborough on March 1, 1888, he played 214 League games for Tottenham Hotspur (1912–23) and 20 for Northampton Town (1926). He also achieved fame as a cricketer – playing in 259 matches for Northamptonshire (1910–29) – but his lasting place in the record books is owed to his diminutive stature. At only 5ft 2in 'Fanny' Walden remains the smallest man to play football for England, being not quite as tall as Shaun

Wright-Phillips, who made his debut in 2004. Walden was originally a moulder in an iron foundry, and stood as umpire in 11 Test matches.

WARREN, BENJAMIN, the England half-back, who from 1899 to 1911 served Derby County and Chelsea, died aged 37 on 15 January, 1917. Born in Newhall, Derbyshire, on May 7, 1879, he rose to national fame – counting 334 League games and 22 caps for his country (1906–11) – but no England international endured a more poignant decline.

On joining Chelsea (1908) he suffered homesickness, so returned each Saturday night to his Derbyshire abode. After sustaining a knee injury he suffered a mental breakdown and retired due to ill health in 1911–12. He began to be plagued by delusions and paranoia, believing he was being poisoned. After being certified insane he entered the Derbyshire Lunatic Asylum, reaching his lowest point when he was found wandering along a Derby street naked except for a collar and tie. He died in Newhall of tuberculosis and was survived by his wife Minnie and four children. Despite his father's vicissitudes, his son Harry became a professional, and in the 1950s proved a good manager to Southend United.

WATTAM, JOHN ARCHIBALD, Sunday footballer extraordinaire, died aged 86 in January 1999 in Lincolnshire, where he was born in 1912. A Grimsby Town enthusiast, he achieved celebrity as 'the oldest footballer in the world'. He began playing as a schoolboy in the 1920s and was still turning out in Sunday League games when in his seventies. In the interim he appeared in over 5,000 matches, playing twice a week until the age of 69, when niggling injuries began to limit his appearances.

For the last 20 seasons of his 60-year career he played for Weelsby Rovers. He joined them when they were in the first division of the local Sunday League, but by 1982 they lay bottom of the tenth, with a forward line whose average age was 50. That season they lost all their 24 games, conceded 234 goals, and scored only 25. In 1983 Jack Wattam won the *Observer* Sports Nut of the Year award, having demonstrated his dedication, aged 71, by playing on Weelsby's right wing only a few days before he went into hospital for a colostomy operation.

WATTS, CHARLES, one of countless men in football with a love of 'the horses', became in November 1924 one of the few to lose his life through that same passion, when he cut his own throat with a razor. Born in Middlesbrough in 1872, Charlie Watts was first goalkeeper (1896–1906) and then trainer (1906–08) at Newcastle United, having played previously for Middlesbrough Ironopolis, Blackburn Rovers and Burton Wanderers. His style both on and off the field was robust. At Blackburn he was suspended after directing a series of insults and abusive remarks to the directors. He was known as a tipster and in a competition organised by the *Sporting Chronicle* in 1898 won the then huge sum of £600.

After 89 League appearances for Newcastle United he pursued his interest in the turf more aggressively. He became a racehorse owner and made and lost his fortune three times. On the final occasion he attempted to clear debts of £3,000 by placing a big bet, but took his own life when the gamble failed. He was 52 and committed the act in the lane running at the back of his home.

WEST, ENOCH JAMES 'KNOCKER', a 'swashbuckling forward' born in Hucknall, Nottinghamshire, on March 31, 1886, went to his grave in 1965 still protesting his innocence over his alleged involvement 50 years earlier in the 'great football betting scandal' of 1915. Along with other players from both sides the Manchester United man had been accused of deliberately fixing the First Division match against Liverpool played at Old Trafford on April 2, 1915 – United emerged 2–0 winners after heavy bets had been placed at odds of 7–1 on that very outcome.

'Knocker' West and seven others were found guilty of contriving the result for personal financial gain. They were banned for life by the Football Association, but after West's seven co-conspirators issued full confessions they were pardoned in 1919 and allowed to continue playing. In contrast West had denied his involvement so vociferously that his own sentence was not lifted until 1945, and even then only as part of a blanket amnesty. The 30-year ban was the longest ever suffered by an English professional, and by the time of his reprieve West was a year short of 60 and too old to resume his career.

He scored 72 goals in 166 League games for Manchester United (1910–15) and had netted 93 previously for Nottingham Forest. After he died aged 79 his cause survived him – through his book *Free the Manchester United One* (2003), Graham Sharpe lobbied the Football Association to grant Enoch West a posthumous pardon, a reasonable request they refused point blank to grant.

WHITTAKER, SPENCE, a promising manager, gave his life in the service of Burnley Football Club, when on Saturday April 16, 1910 he died in Crewe following a mysterious incident aboard a train. He was aged 39 and said to be 'in the prime of his life and the plenitude of his powers'.

Spen Whittaker was born in 1871, at Clayton-le-Moors near Blackburn, and was appointed the first dedicated team manager of Burnley FC in 1903. Having demonstrated an acumen for talent-spotting by signing the legendary goalkeeper Jeremiah 'Jerry' Dawson – whose 569 games for Burnley remain a club record – a buzz went around the town when on Friday April 15, 1910 news broke that Whittaker had signed the talented Accrington player Harry Swift.

Determined to register his capture in time for the next day's home game against Manchester City, the manager boarded the late-night London-bound express train. Between Crewe and Stafford a fellow traveller awoke from his slumber to find that a carriage door was open and that Spen Whittaker had disappeared from the compartment. The Burnley manager was found down the line at Whitmore – alive but suffering from terrible head injuries – and died shortly after midday in Crewe Hospital.

First reports in Burnley told only of 'an accident' – so Harry Swift did not make his debut – and when the news of Whittaker's demise reached the Burnley ground the game was already under way. The Turf Moor flag was immediately lowered to half-mast and an announcement made to the stunned crowd. In a remarkable show of stoicism play was allowed to continue to a conclusion, and against a sombre backdrop the game finished in a three-all draw.

The unexplained death of Spence Whittaker was one of the most tragic events in the whole history of the Football League. A verdict of 'accident' was later given, it being concluded that his fall was neither deliberate nor malicious. He left a wife and three children, who were given the proceeds of a benefit match played at Turf Moor between a Football League XI and Manchester United.

WIDDOWSON, SAMUEL WELLER, the England international centre-forward and devoted servant of Nottingham Forest, died at Beeston, Nottinghamshire, on May 9, 1927, aged 76. Born in Hucknall, near Nottingham, on April 16, 1851, Sam was a fine swimmer, oarsman, cricketer and quarter-miler, and served 'Forest Football Club' (their early incarnation) as both player (1866–85) and long-term committee member. He won one cap for England (1880) and at cricket was selected once for Nottinghamshire (1878), scoring 15 runs in two innings. In Wickets and Goals (1926) the football writer James Catton (q.v.) labelled him 'a hefty athlete,

game as a cock, quite a "card" in his way, and one of the finest forwards of his day'.

By trade a manufacturer of fine lace he was besides an innovator. In 1874 he invented, wore and patented the first shin guard.
Adapted from a cricket pad, it comprised strips of bamboo cane
encased in fabric, strapped to the bare leg or worn outside the
stockings. Although initially derided, the protectors were first
mentioned in Association Laws in 1880, and shin guards are now
officially designated a compulsory item of equipment, and manu-
factured in their millions.

Widdowson was also credited with introducing at Forest in
the 1870s the new 2-3-5 formation – two full-backs, three half-
backs and five forwards – which thereafter remained the standard
tactical line-up for over 70 years. His distinctive forename combination was expressly bestowed by his father Levi, a butcher and
later rent collector, who much admired Charles Dickens' *Pickwick
Papers*, and in particular Mr Pickwick's jovial manservant 'Sam
Weller'.

WILSON, JAMES HAROLD, BARON WILSON OF RIEVAULX, OBE, one
of the most prominent British politicians of the 20th century, died
in London on May 24, 1995, aged 79. He was twice Labour Prime
Minister (1964–70 and 1974–76) and the first premier consciously
to invoke a love of football for political effect. Harold Wilson was
born in Huddersfield on March 11, 1916, and habitually professed
his support of Huddersfield Town, who in his youth were League
Champions three times in a row (1924–26). After England
became World Champions in 1966, Wilson mischievously said:
'Have you noticed how we only win the World Cup under a
Labour government?'

Prior to the 1970 World Cup in Mexico, with a June election
imminent, Wilson personally intervened when the England captain Bobby Moore was arrested in Bogotá, Colombia, on spurious

theft charges – directed by the Prime Minister, British diplomats leant heavily on Colombian officials to secure Moore's release. Four days after England were beaten by West Germany in the quarter-finals, Labour surprisingly lost the General Election, and Wilson expressed the firm opinion that the two disasters were linked. In 1974 he said rather worryingly, 'I know more about football than I do about politics.'

The *Encyclopedia of British Football* (2002) relates that Wilson carried a photograph of Huddersfield's 1926 League Championship-winning side in his wallet, often showing it to visiting dignitaries. Unfortunately a Russian general, who mistakenly thought Wilson wanted his autograph, defaced it.

Harold Wilson suffered Alzheimer's disease in later life and died of colon cancer. He was survived by his wife, the former Gladys Mary Baldwin, and is buried on St Mary's in the Isles of Scilly, the couple's favourite holiday haunt.

WILSON, WALTER BARTLEY, widely known as 'Bart', was a disabled lithographic artist from Bristol whose death at the age of 84 on Friday November 19, 1954 was reported in the *South Wales Echo* headlined 'The Grand Old Man of Cardiff City'. The Welsh club played their first ever game on 7 October, 1899 as Riverside FC, an amateur offshoot of the Riverside Cricket Club, and in little more than a decade they were to become the fully professional outfit known as Cardiff City.

Only by the sterling efforts of Bart Wilson – according to the *Western Mail* he 'beavered, badgered and bullied with imagination and persistence' – was the fledgling Riverside club transformed into a football entity able to upstage rugby's pre-eminence in South Wales.

Wilson served the club in an administrative capacity long into retirement, but his final passage to mortality was not without incident. On the day of his funeral a torrential thunderstorm flash-flooded the graveyard, causing Wilson's coffin to float beside his designated plot and the postponement of the sombre occasion to the following day, when the headstone scheduled to be engraved (already carrying the name of his late wife Sarah Ellen) was mislaid.

Remarkably, the slab was rediscovered 45 years later by club historian Grahame Lloyd, and on June 7, 1999 a re-dedication ceremony was held at Plot 246 of Cardiff's Western Cemetery. Under Wilson's newly engraved name was the simple legend 'The Founder of Cardiff City AFC'. Bart Wilson was no less fêted in more understated times – his entry in the *Football Leader Who's Who* for 1935 read:'Although he walks on crutches he knows football from A–Z' – and as a mark of respect his name has been perpetuated into the 21st century in the form of the Cardiff City mascot Bartley the Bluebird.

WITTGENSTEIN, LUDWIG JOSEF JOHANN, the Austrian philosopher born in Vienna on April 26, 1899, died of prostate cancer on April 29, 1951. Although his abstract theories seldom diverted the football fraternity at large he has been warmly embraced by the burgeoning cottage industry first launched in the 1970s which continues to make footballers of philosophers.

According to his own word the premise of his posthumously published major work *Philosophical Investigations* (1953) was inspired by a football match he had seen when at Cambridge University. Observing the game's ebb and flow, its changing patterns, and the curious mix of strict rules and ready innovation, he likened the players' use of the ball to the way in which language can be employed in philosophical argument to winning effect. The resulting theory he coined 'language-games' has since been intensely debated throughout the world.

His credentials are further bolstered by his selection to represent Germany at the 1972 Munich Olympics in an 'International

Philosophy' match against the Greeks – for the benefit of a *Monty Python* sketch. The line-up – Leibniz, Kant, 'Nobby' Hegel (captain), Schopenhauer, Schelling, Beckenbauer ('obviously a bit of a surprise there'), Jaspers, Schlegel, Wittgenstein, Nietzsche and Heidegger – has become one of the great fantasy teams in football history.

Both sets of players spent the game in deep rumination without threatening either goal until a moment of inspiration by Archimedes created the opening for Socrates to head a late Greek winner. Wittgenstein had by then been substituted by Karl Marx. His death aged 52 occurred at the house of his doctor in Cambridge.

WODEHOUSE, SIR PELHAM GRENVILLE, the famous novelist, who died in hospital on Long Island, New York, on February 14, 1975 at the age of 93, was allotted his obituary in *Wisden* on the strength of a dalliance with cricket. By a similar token he is acknowledged here for his candidacy as the first noted writer of fiction to incorporate association football into his narratives.

His short story *Petticoat Influence* (1906) concerns the hearty doings of the Oxford University soccer team, in which their fleeting encounter with Wolverhampton Wanderers is followed by a stirring description of a Varsity match against Cambridge. The denouement relies on a mix-up caused by the use of the word 'football' to describe both soccer and rugby, at that time a pervasive habit of which the author himself was often guilty.

In *Psmith in the City* (1910) Wodehouse sagely anticipates the idiosyncrasies of fandom through the fickle character Mr Rossiter – head of the postage department at the New Asiatic Bank in London – who is an ardent follower of Manchester United. The same book includes the quaint exclamation 'Play Up the Arsenal!', which literary detectives consider to be the earliest use in popular fiction of a football phrase now universal in its shortened form.

Wodehouse also penned the first ever story concerning football memorabilia. In *The Goal Keeper and Plutocrat* (1912) two rival collectors vie shamelessly for the greatest prizes known to the game, the pair of boots in which Steve Bloomer (q.v.) first played for England and the rubber ball with which Welsh international Billy Meredith practised as a child – this occasion was also the first time real-life professional footballers appeared in a fictional plot.

'The Father of Football Fiction' may be too fanciful an epitaph, but P.G. Wodehouse takes his place as a tentative pioneer of that rarefied literary genre yet to reach its zenith. He was not noted for any personal skill as a footballer.

WOLLASTON, CHARLES HENRY REYNOLDS, an inside-right born at Felpham Vicarage, Sussex, on July 31, 1849, died in London on June 22, 1926, aged 76. It was written that 'he guides the leather with consummate skill', and his tally of five FA Cup-winning medals is a record shared with the Hon. A.F. Kinnaird (q.v.) and James Forrest of Blackburn Rovers. Wollaston gained the honour first, all his triumphs being with Wanderers (1872–78).

After an education at Lancing College and Oxford University he became first a solicitor and later a bank secretary. Although his four England appearances (1874–80) earned him some celebrity his contemporary obituary suggests him to be the least affable England international of all time:

> He shrank from any form of public appearance, and never had his photograph taken except for his passport. He never spoke in public and never spoke about himself at all. He had no liking for society, and his pleasantest hours were spent wandering in the Alps with Swiss guides. He had strong affections for his family, for the hills, music and the sea, but also had a hearty hatred for

particular kinds of men, life and food – aversions which were as violent as they were whimsical and prejudiced. He was firm of purpose and determined to the point of obstinacy.

He never married and in his will left a lifetime annuity to his housekeeper Mrs Parsons and the sum of £100 each to Joseph Biner and Augustin Gentinetta – 'my faithful guides in Switzerland'. He was cremated at Golders Green.

YOUNG, ALEXANDER SIMPSON, the former Everton front man, who died on September 17, 1959, was the first football legend whose trouble in handling retirement led him to fall seriously foul of the law. Born in Slamannan, Stirlingshire, on June 23, 1880, he was twice capped for Scotland (1905–07) but earned his lasting celebrity at Everton (1901–10). Through his scoring of the only goal in the 1906 Cup Final victory over Newcastle United, the Cup was taken to Merseyside for the first time. Young became a prolific marksman and his 28-goal haul the following season won him the English First Division's top scorer accolade. By the time he left Everton he had scored 125 goals in 314 League and FA Cup games.

After unproductive spells with Tottenham Hotspur and Manchester City he left England in 1914 for Australia and was charged there in December 1915 with the wilful murder of his brother. Although found guilty in June 1916 of the lesser charge of manslaughter, his three-year term of imprisonment was later extended because of his 'mental weakness' – his cause not being helped by the English FA officials who all too eagerly attested that during his playing days Young had been prone to 'bouts of temporary insanity'.

In time the saga endured a wild metamorphosis. The television presenter and former England striker Gary Lineker once chirpily told viewers that the wild Scot had been 'hanged for rustling sheep in Australia after the goals dried up'. The truth is more prosaic – Sandy Young returned to his homeland and passed away there aged 79 in the quiet seaside resort of Portobello, near Edinburgh.